ALTERNATIVE FUTURES FOR WORSHIP
Christian Marriage

ALTERNATIVE FUTURES FOR WORSHIP

Volume 5
Christian Marriage

Volume Editor

BERNARD COOKE

Authors

KATHLEEN FISCHER
THOMAS HART
BERNARD COOKE
WILLIAM ROBERTS

THE LITURGICAL PRESS
Collegeville, Minnesota 56321

ISBN 0-8146-1497-3

1   2   3   4   5   6   7   8

Library of Congress Cataloging-in-Publication Data

Alternative futures for worship.

Includes bibliographies.

Contents: v. 1. General Introduction / volume editor, Regis A. Duffy ; authors, Michael A. Cowan, Paul J. Philibert, Edward J. Kilmartin — v. 2. Baptism and confirmation / edited by Mark Searle ; by Andrew D. Thompson . . . [et al.] — v. 3. The eucharist / edited by Bernard J. Lee ; by Thomas Richstatter . . . [et al.] — [etc.]

1. Sacraments (Liturgy) 2. Catholic Church—Liturgy. I. Lee, Bernard J., 1932–
BX2200.A49   1987   265   86-27300
ISBN 0-8146-1491-4 (set)

CONTENTS

The Contributors   7

Preface
    Bernard J. Lee, S.M.   9

Introduction: Christian Marriage
    Bernard Cooke   11

1. The Contemporary Setting for Marriage:
Sociobehavioral Insights
    Kathleen Fischer and Thomas Hart   15

2. Historical Reflections on the Meaning of Marriage
    as Christian Sacrament
    Bernard Cooke   33

3. Theology of Christian Marriage
    William Roberts   47

RITUALS

Practical Liturgical Suggestions for a Wedding Celebration
    and for Family Liturgies: The Wedding Celebration
    Kathleen Fischer and Thomas Hart   69

Liturgy for Celebrating Christian Marriage
    Kathleen Fischer and Thomas Hart   73

A Sample Family Liturgy:
Celebration of Presence
    William Roberts   83

Index   87

THE CONTRIBUTORS

BERNARD COOKE is professor of theology at the College of the Holy Cross, Worcester, Massachusetts.

KATHLEEN FISCHER is an author, geriatric counselor, and theologian in Seattle.

THOMAS HART is an author, pastoral counselor, and theologian in Seattle.

WILLIAM ROBERTS is professor of religious studies at the University of Dayton.

PREFACE

Alternative Futures for Worship is not a product. It is rather a window through which a relationship may be observed. Or to change the image, it is a listening device with which a conversation may be overheard. The participants are sacramental theology, liturgical experience, and the human sciences.

All of life—like all the world—has the possibility of mediating the transformative encounter between God and human history. That is its sacramental character. In the Roman Catholic tradition there has evolved over a long history a system of seven sacraments. These are not our only sacramental experiences. But they occupy a privileged sacramental role in the life of this Christian community.

Each sacrament concerns itself with the religious meanings of some important slice of human life. There are not many slices of life whose patterns and interpreted meanings have not been probed and described by the human sciences. It is crucial, therefore, that sacramental and liturgical theology pay very careful attention indeed to the deliverances of the human sciences. Religious experience cannot, of course, be reduced to the descriptive reports of the human sciences. Yet it would be foolhardy to theologize or "liturgize" apart from serious consideration of these many empirical attempts to understand the character of lived experience in our culture and our time.

Each volume in this series exemplifies the processes of encounter between sacrament, liturgy, and the human sciences: what reports from the human sciences are being considered; how do these understandings affect the meaning structure of the sacrament; how would these meanings find liturgical expression. Every volume in the series has this fundamental agenda, but each takes it up in its own particular way. Our aims are modest; we have not intended to produce any exactly right conclusion. We only care to engage in serious, imaginative, and highly responsible conversation.

It may seem that proposing alternative sacramental rituals is irresponsible, and it would be if they were proposed for anyone's actual use. They are not! This is not an underground sacramentary. We are most aware of the tentative and groping character of each of these attempts.

However, we believe with William James that the best way to understand what something means (like this conversation between Christian experience and the human sciences) is to see what difference it makes. James says you must set an idea to work in the stream of experience to know what it means. We choose ritual as that stream of experience.

Sacramental rituals are not themselves the sacraments. The sacraments are temporally thick slices of life which through time mediate religious experience. The liturgical rite is but one moment in this thicker-than-rite sacramentalization of life. It is a privileged moment though. Ritual is a moment of high value if it illuminates and intensifies the meaning of sacrament. Leonard Bernstein's "Mass for Theatre" speaks movingly of the absurdity of ritual when it has lost touch with the lives of the people who are supposed to be celebrating it. When private meanings and public ritual meanings do not intersect (which is not to say coincide), the absurdity is thundering.

Because a ritual puts a sacramental understanding under the spotlight, we have elected to explore the conversation between sacramental life and the human sciences by imagining ritual appropriations of the fruits of the conversation. That is our way of setting an idea to work imaginatively in the stream of experience. That, and nothing more! But that is a lot.

We suggest that any readers of this volume who have not done so read the introductory volume. There we have tried to say more fully what we think we are about in this entire series and why the many authors who contributed to it are convinced that this project is a quite right thing to do. We are happy to have you listen in on our conversation. Our long-term hope is that you may join it.

Bernard J. Lee, S.M.
San Antonio, Texas

INTRODUCTION: CHRISTIAN MARRIAGE

Bernard Cooke

When the proposal to help edit *Alternative Futures for Worship* was first mentioned, I had reached a certain stage in my own reflection about Christian sacraments. I realized that in many ways marriage, not baptism, was the first sacramental context into which the children of Catholic parents were introduced. Furthermore the sacramentality of marriage and the family remained the dominant lifelong context of most Christians' faith. If that is true, then we face an immense task of educating married couples and families to the sacramental richness of their life together, and in that educational task liturgy would have to play a key role.

So, despite misgivings about the possibility of devising new liturgical forms that would not only honor but actually emerge from our contemporary experience of marriage and family and from social scientific analyses of that experience, I agreed to assemble a team willing to tackle the task. Reaching that agreement was easier than the assembling. What was needed was a group that represented diverse expertise in the behavioral and social sciences, in theology, in history, and in liturgy. But each member of that group would also have to have some insight into each of these specializations. Beyond that a more basic need was for a group for whom marriage was a lived Christian experience that they were able to articulate.

As things worked out, four of us did form a working group and over the months composed, criticized, revised, supplemented, and finally agreed upon the contents of this volume. We see our chapters and suggested liturgies as only a beginning, a very limited approach to Christian marriage as sacrament. It is limited by the practical need of choosing rather arbitrarily to do a few things and to leave many other things undone.

After discussing a wide range of liturgies that might take account of today's multiple concerns surrounding marriage—for example, the changed nature and rhythm of courtship, the widespread breakdown of marriages, the increasing recognition of the equality of women and with it the changing view of roles within the family, the large numbers of divorced and remarried Catholics—we decided that the most worthwhile thing to concentrate on was an appropriate wedding liturgy. Deciding what to do about family liturgies was more of a problem. Prayer should fit the people who pray, and as each family group is distinct, it needs to pray together in a distinctive way. Finally we settled on a list of suggestions for Christian celebrations in the home and provided just one illustration, trusting that interested families would be stimulated to proceed imaginatively on their own.

In preparing the theoretical essays and the suggested liturgies, the team could draw from several areas of specialized expertise. Tom Hart and Kathy Fischer, professionally trained in the social and behavioral sciences as well as theology, are presently engaged in social work and counseling and also teaching theology and writing. Their own marriage, along with their professional work, has given their writings a solid grounding in experience. Much the same is true of Bill Roberts, married and the father of three preteen daughters, whose teaching at the University of Dayton in Dayton, Ohio, and writing have for sometime focused on the theology of Christian marriage. My own long-term interest in Christian sacraments fitted naturally into the project. For many years I had been convinced of the need to understand sacraments in a more human fashion and then find forms of liturgical celebration that would flow from such understanding. In today's world that means drawing from the immense resources of the social and behavioral sciences. We need to see how symbols shape human perception and behavior and how a transformation of key symbols by the significance of Jesus' death and resurrection would change Christians' lives and human society in a revolutionary way.

Our work together was exciting but humbling. Trying to provide liturgical guidance for married couples in today's Church made us more aware how extensive are the needs and challenges these couples face, needs and challenges that social scientific studies have helped us identify but that only faith and trust—in God and in one another—can help us meet. Our hope is that our chapters and liturgical suggestions will make some contribution to a deepened practical understanding of Christian marriage that couples so sorely need. Only out of such understanding and out of the attempt to apply it to life will truly creative and effective sacramental symbols emerge. Liturgy cannot be made; it must be born.

1. THE CONTEMPORARY SETTING FOR MARRIAGE: SOCIOBEHAVIORAL INSIGHTS

Kathleen Fischer and Thomas Hart

Christian marriage in the West exists in a quite different cultural context than it did even a generation ago. A number of developments changes the matrix within which marriage is chosen and lived out. These developments need to be taken into account in the preparation for marriage, the celebration of the marital covenant, and the ongoing support extended to couples. This chapter explores some of the principal sociobehavioral currents influencing marriage today.

Constant Change as a Fact of Life

Until recently our outlook on reality was that what was unchanging was primary and normative and that change was incidental and secondary. This view, rooted in the philosophy of Aristotle, has been challenged by our contemporary experience in which change is seen to permeate all aspects of reality. Darwin's evolutionary findings were the beginning of a revolution in our thinking, which has since been well articulated in the process philosophy of Alfred North Whitehead and the writings of Pierre Teilhard de Chardin and further developed by the schools which they have inspired. Because these ideas are so basic to all that is presented here, let us take a moment to sketch them.

Whitehead has helped us realize that we are confronted with a dynamic rather than a static reality. For example, it is inaccurate to speak of "human nature" as if it were an entity that could be described in categories of substance—if by substance we mean immutable and unchanging thing. The human person is "on the move," a living, changing, developing creature. The dynamic quality of human existence must be recognized and grasped, even if it is also a fact that through all the changes there are persistent qualities which preserve one's identity as human. Likewise the world of nature is not a static affair, but an evolving, changing process. Down to the lowest levels of matter, there is a capacity for and presence of change and development. The world as a whole is *in* process and is *a* process; it is not a finished and settled system composed of discrete entities which are inert, changeless, static.

Besides change the world has a second dominant characteristic. It is an interrelated society of "occasions," Whitehead's dynamic term for realities. Into each of the given occasions, there enter past events as well as the surrounding and accompanying pressures of other occasions, not to mention the lure of the future. Human persons, for example, are all that have gone to make them up, all that surround them, all that press upon them, all that they themselves enter into and in which they share, all which they may be. We live in and are confronted by a richly interconnected, interrelated, interpenetrative series of events, just as we ourselves are such a series of events. Thus change and relation are the two main themes of process thought, as they are the two key elements of fully realized experience.

Teilhard de Chardin, who thought independently along these same lines, articulated a vision of cosmic evolution from its most elemental beginning stages all the way to the future culmination of history in the second coming of Christ. Working on a very broad canvas constituted of both scientific and theological elements, he worked to make Christian theological understanding commensurate with the vision of the cosmos which the twentieth century has given us. Teilhard too stresses the constantly evolving, developmental process in which all things are involved and particularly the growing interrelatedness of human beings as they gradually come to the full stature of the body of Christ. The full development of that body is the goal of history, the omega point, the second coming.

It is not our purpose here to do any kind of justice to the full complexity of the thought of either of these two seminal thinkers. We call attention to them simply because the kind of philosophical and theological thinking they are engaged in so well articulates the contemporary experience of reality as constantly evolving and intimately interrelated.

Among the many effects of this shift in our experience and thought is a changed perspective on the life of the human person. We see the person now as self-creating, as unfolding step-by-step through the many stages of the life cycle. Erik Erikson laid out these stages in the 1960's, and his scheme caught the popular interest, particularly as it pertained to child and adolescent development. In the 1970's Gail Sheehy in *Passages* and Daniel Levinson in *The Seasons of a Man's Life* focused on adult development and on the particular tasks and opportunities of the twenties, thirties, and forties, all the way to the final years of the life cycle. In this perspective all of life is seen to be developmental, and our maturation as human beings is open-ended from birth to death. In the process everyone and everything that we interact with are crucially formative.

In the present decade the marital therapist Mel Krantzler has presented a view of marriage itself along developmental lines. The thesis of his *Creative Marriage* is that just as the life of the individual goes through stages of growth, each with its peculiar challenges and opportunities, so does the life of a marriage. Within every marriage, Krantzler holds, there are six marriages, succeeding each other over time. First there is the laying of the foundations in the early years. Then come the child-bearing years. Sometime in the course of these comes the establishing of careers. Then gradually there is the emptying of the nest. Next comes the adjustment to retirement. Finally there is the movement toward death and then the acceptance of death itself. At every stage of their life together, a couple has to make a new covenant in accordance with their changing circumstances, recreating the marriage anew on the basis of changed tasks, needs, and aspirations.

While these personal and interpersonal developments are taking place, the culture is also changing. And the speed with which the culture changes seems to accelerate as time goes on. Within the nine decades of the twentieth century, there has probably been more change in cultural patterns in the West than there was in the preceding thirty decades. The growth of science and its application in a vast array of technological achievements have transformed and continue to transform our whole way of life.

If we look at developments in just two areas, transportation and communication, the present century has seen the birth of both the automobile and the airplane, of radio, television, and finally the computer. The ease of transportation has resulted in tremendous mobility with the resultant mixing of cultures and exchange of goods. The speed of communication puts us in touch with what is happening all around the globe, fosters much more mutual influence, and results in something quite new in the history of humankind: world consciousness as a more or less habitual state of mind. In this tightly interlocked and highly industrialized world, new ideas, new methods, and new devices are spawned at such a rapid rate that all arrangements come to be experienced as provisional, awaiting further developments. This is a very different world than our ancestors lived in. It is even different from the world of our parents and certainly our grandparents. They knew much more stability and lived their lives at a more leisurely pace. The present century has seen the invention and development of the phonograph record and cassette tape, the camera, the automatic washer and dryer, the copying machine, the microwave oven, the fast food restaurant, the shopping center, the freeway, the rocket, and radar. It has also enjoyed the benefits of immense progress in medical science. Our way of life has been revolutionized, and developments are likely to continue at an even more rapid rate.

Even the Roman Catholic Church has changed and is changing, to the surprise of many. For the Church, above all, was thought to be the bastion of stability and timeless truth. This impression was largely the result of the illusion which makes us think that the way things are is the way they have always been. Historical research shows very clearly that Church doctrine, liturgical practice, and political structure are all products of historical evolution. Once this truth is grasped, it becomes obvious how these same realities must continue to be updated and adapted to meet the challenges of ever changing times and cultures.

Given our increased awareness of how the individual changes throughout the life cycle, how marriage itself undergoes stress at all the critical junctures of its ongoing development, and how the values and practices of the surrounding culture continue to evolve, people today are reluctant to make permanent commitments. The divorce rate is already high (nearly fifty percent of marriages), and many people of marriageable age have experienced the pain of divorce at close hand. This introduces a marked hesitancy. To live in the West today is to be accustomed to moving geographically, to holding a succession of jobs, to relating to a changing circle of friends, to being bombarded with a confusing variety of philosophies and values. Having learned to expect and to live flexibly with change, many people experience a strong reluctance to enter into a lifetime commitment to another individual in marriage. Even where such commitments are made, people have increased difficulty remaining faithful to them.

Perhaps the most fitting overarching theological motif for expressing the experience of marriage today is that of death and resurrection. At each of its difficult passages, a marriage needs to die so that it can live again. It must let go of what is familiar so that it can move into a genuinely different future. The Christian mystery of death and resurrection captures the threat and pain of this experience as well as the hope that sustains it. It expresses both genuine transformation and underlying continuity.

An Organic View of Marriage and Family Relationships

The prevailing model in the sociological analysis of marriage and family relationships is the systems model, which sees the family, with or without children, as an organism of interdependent and interacting parts. It is not a mere collectivity of individuals whose association with each other is secondary to their individuality. The mutual influence is recognized to be so strong that it becomes constitutive of the development of each of the individuals who are part of the whole. This conforms to the Whiteheadian insight, elaborated in *Process and Reality*, that relationships are not mere accidents added on, as it were, from the outside, but are constitutive of the very reality of anything. We are formed by the people we relate to. They become part of us.

The strength of family interrelatedness became manifest in the 1950's when psychotherapists began to see whole families instead of just the member of the family who was designated as mentally ill. Watching the family members interact with one another, the therapists developed new hypotheses about the genesis and maintenance of mental illness. They now understood how the whole family was involved in the patient's problems. The new perspective was confirmed by the fact that when the sick person who had been hospitalized became well and was reinserted into the family, the troublesome symptoms often returned. The entire family needed to change.

These discoveries revolutionized the field of marriage and family therapy and introduced social awareness even into individual therapy. The assumption of psychoanalysis had been that the mentally sick person had deep-seated problems rooted either in physiology or in the psyche and that the person needed intensive individual therapy. If a couple presented themselves as having marriage problems, each was taken singly and psychoanalyzed. A family in distress would put forth their identified patient, and he or she would undergo treatment. The problem was seen to be in the individual and not in the interaction.

Once the idea of observing whole families had caught the imagination of therapists around the country, the family therapy movement leapt forward in several places at once. Among its best known pioneers are Gregory Bateson, Nathan Ackerman, Murray Bowen, Carl Whitaker, Milton Erickson, Salvador Minuchin, Don Jackson, Jay Haley, and Virginia Satir. The history of the whole development and its principal concepts is well summarized in Lynn Hoffman's *Foundations of Family Therapy*. For our present purposes an illustration or two might be most helpful.

A boy of fifteen begins acting out in school. He disrupts order in the classroom, stops turning in assignments, starts a fire in a school locker. The parents send him to a counselor. The counselor calls in the whole family. As the family presents itself, it becomes obvious that there are serious problems between the parents. They cannot agree on much of anything. They bicker constantly, and the marriage is always threatening to break up. The boy has discovered that when he acts out, it serves to pull his parents together at least temporarily to deal with his problems. Without fully realizing it, he is sacrificing himself to hold the family together.

What the family therapy movement has shown about family pathology is true also of family health and growth. All members of the family are intimately coinvolved and influence each other. A couple or family is something like a mobile. If you touch any part of a mobile, you move all the parts. In a family the behavior of each member affects all the others. If the wife and mother takes a job outside the home, all the members of the family are affected and have to make adaptive changes. If either parent becomes unemployed, there is a similar total impact. As a child moves from grade school to high school and begins new associations and activities, all members of the family are affected in various ways. If a family member is moving through a difficult period and becomes depressed, the life of the whole family organism is profoundly affected.

When family life goes well, family members create one another, affirm and support one another, heal and free one another. Husband and wife work on their own personal growth, not just for their own sake but for the sake of spouse and children too, as the impact for good or ill is so great. In the context of Christian faith, family members are mediators of God's own gracious action in each other's lives. As they challenge and comfort one another, husband and wife are instruments of the shaping action of God on one another and their children. Once this is grasped, it is easily seen how much more is at stake in a marriage than a contractual arrangement to realize certain practical advantages.

This sociobehavioral insight ties in well with the theological realization that wife and husband are called to love one another as Christ loves his people, that is, in accepting, supportive, forgiving, healing, freeing, and nurturing ways. The kind of loving that is called for is seen in Jesus' ministry to people, and its consequences are evident there too.

Family of Origin as Formative Influence

Even after an individual has left the matrix of family and begun an independent life, he or she carries the formative influence of that family as a permanent endowment. Not only is it part of one's genetic makeup, it is the deepest part of one's cultural formation as well. Usually there is ongoing contact with members of one's family of origin which keeps the relationships and their ramifications very much alive. And often enough even after the death of one's parents, one is still unconsciously involved in pleasing them or rebelling against them.

When one marries, one marries not just an individual but the individual's family as well, both in the sense that they are stamped upon the individual and that there will continue to be interaction with them as long as they live. Let us look briefly at each of these kinds of influence.

Our families are the source of many of the gifts and strengths we bring to marriage. They are also at the root of some of the things from which we struggle to free ourselves. Much of this is not in full awareness when we marry, but it comes to awareness through the unfolding of marital interaction. It is usually our spouses who remind us that we are just like our mothers or fathers, because we do tend to repeat the patterns of life in which we were raised, sometimes despite strong resolutions to the contrary. We tend to solve problems the way we saw them solved, express affection the way we saw it expressed, deal with anger the way we saw it dealt with, treat children the way we were treated. If we have unfinished business with mother or father, we tend to try to finish it with wife or husband. If we were loved for who we were, we tend to love ourselves and to love our new mate for the persons we are. If we saw healthy patterns of interaction between parents, we tend to exhibit healthy patterns in our own interaction. What happened long ago bestows the blessings and sets the growth tasks for the present marriage. An illustration from marriage counseling might serve to make this clear.

A man comes in for counseling with his wife. The problem is that he is habitually angry in the marriage, and his outbursts at slight provocations are extremely hard on his wife, who feels she can no longer take a chance on getting close. The course of counseling brings out the fact that as a boy of seven, the husband was abandoned by his father, who left the home. The stepfather who replaced the father never loved the boy and treated him harshly. As husband and father now the man feels deeply inadequate by reason of his childhood deprivations. He has had no model to teach him how to relate to wife and children. His feelings of inadequacy and of resentment at not having had a father's love lie at the root of his habitual anger. Therapy and other constructive influences in his life can help him to a considerable extent with his problem, but growth is gradual, and his wife and children must bear some of the marks of what has happened to him.

Then there is the whole matter of ongoing interaction with parents. There are letters, calls, and visits back and forth. There are expectations which gradually become known: expectations touching holidays, grandchildren, sometimes even jobs and style of life. These have to be dealt with. Sometimes we are called upon to give financial assistance to our parents in their later years, to help out a brother or sister in crisis, to offer temporary or permanent residence. In these and other ways our relationships with family members continue to have a major impact on our marriage. We experience in this both great blessings and considerable challenges.

Here again we see how significant our community linkages are. There is human solidarity in sin and its effects, and there is solidarity in grace and its effects. Our perspective on marriage today cannot but be affected by our growing insight into the deep and pervasive effects of our communication with one another.

A New Understanding of the Relationship Between the Sexes

Just a generation or two ago the relationship between the sexes was quite clearly defined in terms of hierarchy and complementarity. Regarding the first, the man was head of the woman and of the household. This conviction was clearly symbolized in the nuptial rite itself in the father's action of handing over his daughter to her future husband. This part of the rite goes back to ancient Rome, where the conception was that women were owned by their fathers and husbands, and the ritual enacted an exchange of property. If today it seems a harmless and relatively meaningless ritual, the best way to realize that it conveys considerable meaning is to imagine the mother handing over her son to the bride. That action would almost certainly draw protests. Asking the groom to take the bride's name would make the same point and probably elicit a similar reaction. The sexism inherent in the ancient Roman practice can invoke biblical texts in its support and often has in the history of the Church. The Genesis account of the creation of the woman from the man's rib to be his helpmate (Gen 2:18-25) and the statements in Ephesians that the husband is head of his wife and that wives should obey their husbands in all things (Eph 5:21-24) are among the biblical statements cited. What Scripture scholars realize today is that the sexism of a patriarchal society was simply taken for granted and comes through in these texts, not as part of God's inspired message but as part of the cultural framework in which that message was expressed. But until the very recent past, these sexist dictates went for the most part unchallenged. Thus the family was seen as hierarchical: husband over wife over children.

The relationship of the sexes was also seen as complementary with the respective roles clearly defined. The husband was the breadwinner, the wife the homemaker. He was the provider, she the nurturer. His job was to protect, hers to support. He was the voice of reason, she of feeling. His office was in the marketplace, hers in the home. It was for him to initiate, and for her to respond.

The women's movement has challenged the patriarchical ideology and structures of Western society. The emergent understanding views the relationship between the sexes more in terms of mutuality and equality than of hierarchy and complementarity. It resists the stereotyping of the sexes, which it sees as unfairly constricting to each. Sociologist Jesse Bernard has made available the findings of recent research on roles in marriage and family life in her *The*

Future of Marriage and *Women, Wives, Mothers: Values and Options.*

In contemporary understanding and practice women have a legitimate and indeed indispensable place in business, politics, and religion. They often play a major role in the financial support of their families. Men have gifts for homemaking and nurturing and play a larger role than before in cooking, homemaking, and caring for their children. Decision-making is mutual, and the tasks of maintaining home and family are distributed in a variety of ways based on gifts, interests, and opportunities. All of this profoundly affects the expectations with which a couple enters marriage and the style in which they live it out.

If this treatment suggests that the old way was all wrong and the new way correct, it should be said that there have been many successful and happy marriages under the rules of hierarchy and complementarity, and there continue to be. But the challenge of the women's movement has made us aware that it does not have to be this way and that it is not always good for a man and woman to live on such terms.

One of the crises arising in marriages today occurs when a couple who married under the old expectations experiences a change of viewpoint. The wife typically begins to feel confined in too small a world of home and family and too little respected where her judgment and personal freedom are concerned. As she begins to assert herself and move out more, her husband feels threatened in his power, wonders about her love and loyalty, and fears he will lose her. If instead of recognizing and allowing for what is happening, he pushes to maintain the status quo, he often does lose her. But if the couple makes a new covenant, both can look forward to expansion and growth.

A couple came for counseling amidst the stresses of such a transition, without being fully aware of what was going on. The wife had recently returned to school in order to pursue a career. Her school obligations meant there were two nights a week when she did not have dinner on the table as before and one day of the weekend when she was not available for the kinds of activities they had shared in the first ten years of their marriage. The husband showed increasing irritability and criticism. He was also feeling in her new project an uncomfortable challenge to his adequacy as a breadwinner. It took a lot of listening on his part in counseling to begin to grasp that she was not challenging him at all nor was she rejecting him, but that she was feeling stifled in too small a world and needed to expand that world to get some of her needs met. As he changed slowly from opposing her to supporting her in her endeavors, her defensiveness and hostility decreased, their closeness came back, and he and the children began to see how they were benefiting from the richer contribution she was able to make to several dimensions of family life.

If a sexist approach to marriage can find biblical support, so can the freer, more flexible attitude which grows among us today. Scripture scholars are reading the creation accounts in Genesis with deepened insight and reminding us also of what Paul says in Gal 3:28 about the new creation in Christ in which there is neither Jew nor Greek, slave nor free person, male nor female, but all are on an equal footing. Among the consequences of the new perspective is a need to help couples preparing for marriage to talk through what their respective roles and responsibilities will be and to celebrate their marriage in a liturgy free of sexist language and stereotypical expectations.

Higher Marital Expectations

People living in Western culture today expect more of life, of themselves, and of relationships. They live in a society of increasing opportunities. Education is no longer seen as ending with graduation from college in one's early twenties. Colleges and universities serve an ever growing number of people pursuing degrees or at least courses for enrichment all through adult life. The churches have developed ambitious programs in adult education, where before all the energy went into the education and formation of children. In a variety of settings, study groups and growth groups meet around diverse agenda. Bookstores carry an extensive inventory of self-help books. Computer stores exhibit an equal or greater variety of self-education courses for use with home computers. To live is to grow, from birth to death.

People enter marriage today in quest of personal fulfillment. They tend to want more communication, more personal sharing and intimacy, and at the same time more opportunity to pursue fulfillment in activities outside the home. People live considerably longer than before. After a couple have raised their children and sent them on their way, they can look forward to perhaps thirty more years of life together. This is a very different situation from the shorter-term marriages for economic reasons and child rearing which characterized the not too distant past.

There is a richness of opportunity here which is most welcome. There is also a considerable challenge to both members of the marriage. It is no longer enough just to "be there" and to remain sexually faithful to one person. There is a far higher expectation of interpersonal companionship, of support of each other's growth and autonomy, and of flexibility when growth brings change in family life. There are times of great stress as one person's growth outstrips the other's, or one's needs and interests change while the other's remain the same. Husbands are sometimes puzzled when their wives divorce them even though they have been good providers and have never been guilty of infidelity, drunkenness, or violence. Marital expectations today go considerably beyond these things. People leave their marriages today simply because they are bored in the relationship, are disappointed in the lack of interpersonal intimacy, or are not feeling fulfilled.

A woman came for counseling with her husband. She expressed the deepest frustration over his lack of communication with her. He was interested, she said, in his business, sports, and sex, and that was about all. He rarely had anything to say, shared very little of himself, and did not show all that much interest in her and the things that were important to her. She was a great reader and avid socializer and was deeply involved in religious activities. She said he was not a bad man at all, that he was honest, gentle, and faithful, but that he was no companion in all the more profound ways she longed for companionship. For that reason, though it caused her acute pain, she was seriously considering divorcing him. He for his part had always been happy in the marriage and wanted it to continue. He was bothered only by her unhappiness and two of its apparent results: more nagging and less sex. The problem experienced by this couple and the woman's serious consideration of divorce are not at all untypical today. If the marriage is going to survive, both husband and wife must meet the challenge: he to behavioral change, she to greater acceptance of his limitations and creative ways of getting some of her needs met outside the marriage.

As Christians we celebrate the emphasis on married life as opportunity for growth and fulfillment. At the same time we recognize that this thrust can become selfish. We may be better today at teaching people how to make their needs known and get them met than we are at teaching them how to sacrifice for one another, forgive, and persevere with one another in love. But this is another important area for couples' growth in the Christian life, and it deserves some emphasis in the challenge expressed to them in the marriage rite.

A Broader View of Marital Generativity

The present century has witnessed another great revolution. Medical science has quite thoroughly mapped the process of human reproduction and given us a very considerable measure of control over it. One of the developments we still await is the ability to predict the moment of ovulation accurately, but it seems to be only a matter of time before this knowledge too will be gained and our control of the generative process will be still more complete.

Increased knowledge means a larger range of choice. Couples today typically wait longer before having their first child, space their children at greater intervals, and choose to have smaller families. The birthrate in the industrialized countries has fallen sharply. This comes partly from the desire for more personal freedom and a higher standard of living. It reflects the experience of economic pressures and a sense of what it means and costs to raise a child in today's world. But it also stems from a broader view of generativity.

A couple might choose to have few or no children in favor of devoting their time and resources to life-generating activity outside the immediate family circle. They might adopt children not now cared for in families or take in foster children for temporary care until they are placed with families. Generativity takes other forms as well. Just as religious men and women have chosen celibacy to free themselves for service to wider circles of people, a growing number of couples today choose to limit their biological generativity and devote themselves to teaching, writing, social work, counseling, administration, and other ministries to needy people. They see their marriage primarily as a union of companionship and mutual support in the difficult work of ministry and express generativity in their labors to improve the quality of life for others. This creates a different style of marriage and family life than was familiar in the past. If in the past marriage was ever conceived along these lines, it could hardly have been lived out except in a celibate lifestyle, because sex meant reproduction.

Greater Focus on the Relational Aspect of Human Sexuality

Sex was a forbidden subject not too long ago. It was spoken of in secret if it was spoken of at all, and what was said about it was condemning or cautionary rather than affirming. Now human sexuality is a subject of public discussion. Besides the magazine and film industries which exploit it for profit, there is a proliferation of popular books and articles on every aspect of the subject. Religious writing on human sexuality today joins with the secular output in proclaiming that sex is a gift meant to be enjoyed. Where people are experiencing sexual difficulty, professional sex clinics are available to assist them in working out their problems. The methods used in these clinics have themselves become part of the popular literature. Bernie Zilbergeld's *Male Sexuality* and Lonnie Barbach's *For Each Other* are examples of balanced professional approaches to helping people become comfortable with their sexuality and reach greater sexual satisfaction with their partners.

It is the relational aspect of sexuality that is focused on in this whole development. Apart from a relatively small body of literature addressed specifically to couples having trouble with fertility, almost all of this writing simply takes it for granted that couples desiring to have a child need no help in doing so. It focuses instead on improving sexual communication, the premise being that in the vast majority of instances the sexual encounter is for communication, relaxation, and celebration rather than for generation. It is well-known that except for a brief time each month a woman is infertile, even if no measures whatsoever are taken to avoid pregnancy.

The Roman Catholic Church is well known for its emphasis on the procreative aspect of human sexuality. But here too there has been a significant shift. Prior to the Second Vatican Council, the Church insisted that procreation was the primary end of human sexuality, its relational aspect secondary. At the council the Church abandoned this practice of prioritizing and accorded the procreative and relational aspects of sexuality equal importance. All Vatican documents on sexuality since the council have been consistent with this position, further developing a theology of sexuality which accords great significance to human sexuality's power to strengthen the marital bond quite apart from generation.

In the new climate new moral questions arise. Discussion focuses on the appropriateness of sexual expression at mature stages of development in relationships which are headed for marriage. A related question is raised by homosexuals about the appropriateness of sexual expression at similar stages of development in their committed relationships. Not everyone awaits final Church pronouncements in such matters or abides by the pronouncements made. People coming to marriage today come with much more sexual experience and sophistication than their parents had and therefore also with higher expectations. They are much less likely simply to bear with sexual dissatisfaction.

One of the manifestations of the increased interest in the relational aspect of sex is the growing number of couples who seek help for sexual dissatisfaction. Men who have erection problems or ejaculate prematurely seek remedies so that they can enjoy more sexual fulfillment with their partners. Women with orgasmic difficulty ask for help in getting free of whatever is blocking them from full sexual participation and satisfaction. It is not uncommon for wives or husbands to complain about their spouses' apparent lack of interest in having sex with them, a complaint arising both from the sense of missing out on something valuable and from the pain of apparent rejection. Many couples seek help in learning simply to communicate more effectively with one another in the sexual area.

One particular result of our increased knowledge of human sexuality and our open communication about it is the recognition that sexual fulfillment is not just a male but a female interest as well. What had been thought of as pretty exclusively a male domain is now seen as a common domain. Both parties in a marriage have an interest in and a right to sexual satisfaction. Either party might initiate sex, and either party might refuse at given times. Both have to express their needs and wants to each other, letting themselves be known sexually so that they might enjoy the satisfaction that can come only when the relationship is mutually communicative and accommodating.

A New Plurality of Life-styles

There is much greater fluidity of life-styles today than there was a generation or two ago. Then it was expected that nearly everyone would marry upon reaching adulthood. Now there are many more options. The single life-style is much more accepted and more widely chosen. In today's society women as well as men can find careers and satisfying employment and might reject marriage as unattractive to them. Another major social development is the practice of couples living together without permanent commitment. Many seek a much greater test of their viability as a couple actually living together than their parents had before making a permanent commitment. They do not want to hazard such a commitment on the basis of a mere dating relationship. Control of the generative process and a greater social acceptance of unmarried couples living together make this kind of testing a possibility. This new freedom and plurality of life-styles has produced a situation where marriage becomes quite a deliberate choice, a choice among options. Even when it is chosen, other options continue to exercise their attraction, especially when the going becomes difficult.

The idea is not to persuade more people to marry but to support those who have chosen this life-style, particularly since in the context of Christian faith, marriage is the sign of the kind of love with which Christ loves his people. It is a life-giving sign in the Christian community. One of our tasks as Christians is to support couples as they undergo their deaths and resurrections together, so they can experience and be transformed by the saving action of God in the depths of their lives. In a social situation of competing life-styles, it is evident that couples will need more support than before, especially the support of other couples who can affirm the rationale and values of Christian marriage and offer assistance with the challenges it encounters as it unfolds.

The foregoing considerations suggest something of the cultural context in which marriage is undertaken today. They point up a need for good preparation and ongoing support. They also offer several cues for the fashioning of an appropriate marriage liturgy.

Couples entering Christian marriage today need the assistance of the community. They can be helped to scrutinize their expectations at the outset and to bring them into closer conformity with the realities they are likely to encounter. They can be introduced to the typical struggles of marital adjustment, offered suggestions for dealing with them, and made aware of the rewards of staying with a life commitment and growing through its challenges. It is, of course, not just initial preparation but ongoing support that is needed.

Married life needs to be situated within a context of Christian faith and Christian values, the ideal of Christ's love for Christians being held up as the model for a man and woman's love for one another. The struggles of married life can be related to the paschal mystery, where death leads to resurrection and a new quality of life. The working of grace among human beings can be related to the systemic character of family life where the mutual influences are so crucially formative.

But more than a conceptual framework—even a framework of faith—is needed to sustain marriage today. Couples need ongoing interaction with other couples embarked on the same challenging journey, the assistance of professionals who share their faith in times of particular difficulty, and the continual nourishment of the sacramental life of the Church. This initial preparation and ongoing network of support have probably never been more important for Christian married life than they are today.

References

Barbach, Lonnie. *For Each Other: Sharing Sexual Intimacy.* Garden City, N.Y.: Doubleday, 1982. A balanced treatment of human sexuality from the standpoint of the female of the couple, attempting to change negative attitudes and address common problems.

Bernard, Jesse. *The Future of Marriage.* Cleveland: World Books, 1972.

Bernard, Jesse. *Women, Wives, Mothers: Values and Options.* Chicago: Aldine Press, 1975. Sociological surveys of recent research on roles in marriage and family life.

Cobb, Jr., John, and Griffin, David. *Process Theology: An Introductory Exposition.* Philadelphia: Westminster Press, 1976. A brief, clear introduction to process thought and an application of its central notions to several contemporary questions.

Hoffman, Lynn. *Foundations of Family Therapy.* New York: Basic Books, 1981. A comprehensive historical survey of the birth and development of the field of marriage and family therapy.

Kolbenschlag, Madonna. *Kiss Sleeping Beauty Goodbye: Breaking the Spell of Feminine Myths and Models.* New York: Bantam, 1979. A scholarly treatment, with the fairy tales of Western culture as launching point of the oppressive sexism embedded in the culture.

Krantzler, Mel. *Creative Marriage.* New York: McGraw Hill, 1981. A treatment of the course of marriage as unfolding six successive stages, each with its peculiar tasks and opportunities calling for creativity.

Paolini, Thomas, and McCrady, Barbara, eds. *Marriage and Marital Therapy.* New York: Brunner Mazel, 1978. Outlines the perspectives of psychoanalysis, behaviorism, and systems theory in understanding marriage and marriage problems today.

Satir, Virginia. *Peoplemaking.* Palo Alto, Calif.: Science and Behavior Books, 1972. Shows how a family interacts and how each member is shaped by the nature of the interaction, personal growth being either fostered or impeded.

Schwartz, Pepper, and Blumstein, Philip. *American Couples: Money, Work, Sex.* New York: Morrow, 1983. A sociological study of the life patterns of American couples today.

Tufte, Virginia, and Myerhoff, Barbara, eds. *Changing Images of the Family*. New Haven, Conn.: Yale University Press, 1979. Cross-disciplinary scholarship on the changing forms of marriage and family life today.

Whitehead, James and Evelyn. *Marrying Well: Possibilities in Christian Marriage Today*. Garden City, N.Y.: Doubleday, 1981. A broad survey of contemporary trends in marriage. Addresses the many needs of couples today from a Christian perspective.

Zilbergeld, Bernie. *Male Sexuality*. New York: Bantam, 1978. A balanced treatment of male sexuality, exploding myths, cultivating attitudes, solving problems.

2. HISTORICAL REFLECTIONS ON THE MEANING OF MARRIAGE AS CHRISTIAN SACRAMENT

Bernard Cooke

The initial chapter in this fascicle illustrates the ways in which research and reflection in the social and behavioral sciences have given us a clearer understanding of marriage and thereby provided the foundation for a more profound insight into what we have called the Christian sacrament of marriage. This does not mean that women and men of previous generations had little or no accurate grasp of what it meant to be married as Christians. In many cases their Christian faith and their love for one another led them to a deep and correct appreciation of marriage. However, this appreciation was often unformulated, and people lived out their marriage relationship with very little to guide them except their own experience.

One of the most helpful ways of understanding a reality such as Christian marriage is to examine the historical evolution that brought it to its present-day state. Such historical reflection cannot replace the more analytic approach of the social sciences, but it is a valuable complement because it permits people to compare their own situation with that of persons in other times and places. However, there is a basic problem that often makes such historical study difficult if not impossible: before one can trace the history of something, one must know what it is that one is trying to trace.

This problem is very acute in the case of Christian marriage. Surprisingly it is not clear just what constitutes human marriage and even less clear just what constitutes a Christian marriage. For more than two thousand years opinions have differed as to whether a marriage was brought into existence by two persons agreeing to share their lives permanently, or by some public authority recognizing this marital intent of the couple, or by these two people giving to one another exclusive rights to sexual intercourse, or by the act of intercourse itself, or by a couple living together over a considerable period of time, or by one or other contractual agreement between the families of the two persons, or by some combination of these.

To put it quite simply, it has never been perfectly clear who is married and who is not, though there has been rather general recognition that most people in any society live with some other person (or persons) in a marriage.

So what is it whose history we wish to sketch? Without trying to add to the detailed historical studies that have recently appeared,[1] this chapter will attempt to describe briefly three elements of the historical picture. First, what has been the Christian understanding of marriage as a human reality? Second, what has been distinctive about the way Christians became married and the nature of their married relationship? Third, what has been meant by calling Christian marriage a sacrament?

What Is Marriage?

Attempts to study the history of Christian marriage in the earliest periods of the Church's life are immediately stymied by the lack of evidence for anything that could be called specifically Christian. This lack, however, indicates rather clearly that apart from the fact that the two persons involved were Christian, there was nothing noticeably different about Christian marriages, about the way they originated, the way they were lived, or (in some instances) in the way they were terminated.

Ideally the motivations and values that brought a Christian woman and man into a given relationship expressed their Christian faith, and the Gospel perspective deepened their loving concern for one another. But in their external forms and social identification, the marriages of Christians were not discernibly different from the other marriages in society. Christians became married according to the patterns of whatever culture they lived in. Becoming married was seen, in other words, to be a basic human undertaking that Christians did much as others did, though the nature of their relationship to one another might have been touched by their understanding of what it meant for them to be related to one another "in the Lord."

Having said this, we can trace among Christians over the centuries a varying and somewhat diverse understanding of what marriage is. Since the practical context of our understanding is that of Roman Catholic thought and practice, we can concentrate on those developments in Western Christianity that fed into what became the Catholic tradition. Some of the developments in Eastern Christianity and in Protestantism were slightly different, but that need not concern us here.

In its beginning the Christian understanding of human marriage was strongly influenced by the viewpoint of Judaism and then increasingly by the outlook of Roman law and custom. Judaism at the time of Christianity's origin had inherited a fundamentally positive attitude towards human sexuality and for that historical period a rather lofty view of marriage. Marriage was considered a responsibility intrinsic to adult life; one was expected to raise up and educate God-fearing children so that the people Israel could continue and prosper, and God be glorified.

Israel's strongly patriarchal culture still kept women in an inferior position. In marriage the woman was subordinate to her husband and expected to reverence and obey him as her lord. She did not have the rights he possessed regarding divorce, and she was bound by a stricter rule of marital fidelity than he. It was the man who took the woman in marriage, quite literally. She passed from the jurisdiction and care of her father to that of her husband. Being married for a woman was a matter of changing households and roles within the household.

Yet there was a definite tradition of marriage being a relationship of love between the spouses. The Canticle of Canticles bears witness to this tradition. Marriage arrangements were still a matter of negotiations between families, but it seems that the preferences of the young persons involved, particularly the young man, were often as not honored. Israel's key religious category, covenant, was used as a way of describing the marriage agreement, and the prophetic imagery that used marriage as metaphor of Yahweh's relation to his people gave marriage special moral and religious endorsement.

Rome's most ancient cultural traditions involved great respect for family and marriage as the key to tribal continuity. As elsewhere in the ancient world, marriages—at least in the upper classes—were arranged for the young couple, but the marriage it-self was seen to consist essentially in the two people consenting to stable cohabitation. Marriage was a family affair; the only involve-ment of the state concerned questions of property or public respon-sibility.

Christianity's earliest generations, then, would have regarded marriage much as did diaspora Judaism. Christians would have seen marriage as an arrangement between two people who wished to share life and establish their own household. Marital sexuality would have been taken for granted as intrinsic to this arrangement and sexual fidelity as a basic responsibility of each spouse. Christians would not have regarded their marriage as anything distinctively related to their Christian faith. They would have believed, however, that their regard for and relationship to one another in a marriage had a special character, because Christian marriage, and especially the sexual union of woman and man, was meant to mirror the love that linked Christ and his Church.

By the year 200, however, a negativity towards human sexual-ity infiltrated Christianity and began to limit Christians' positive esteem for marriage, so much so that "family" ceased to be a primary model for thinking about the Church. One must be careful not to judge Christians' attitude towards their own individual marriages simply by the statements of those theologians and bishops we call "Fathers of the Church," but those statements do reflect much of the current outlook. Reading those Patristic judgments on mar-riage, one is appalled by the shift in outlook that has occurred. Though they still pay homage to the notion that marriage is good because established by God and related to Christ's love for the Church, the Fathers see marriage as seriously "wounded" because it entails sexual intercourse.

In their view procreation of children for the next generation of Christians is the only thing that truly legitimates marital intercourse. Sexual relations without such an objective are a concession to hu-man carnality, only somewhat legitimated by the fact that sexual activity within marriage is an outlet that keeps a man from the greater evil of extramarital promiscuity. All such considerations of marriage deal, of course, only with the man's situation, the "prob-lems" that sexuality and women present for him, whether in or out-side marriage. Implicitly, at times explicitly, the human dignity and Christian spirituality of a married woman are denigrated.

Besides, during the Patristic period (roughly 200 to 600) monasticism became a widespread phenomenon in the life of the Church. Such a way of life, which allowed a Christian to "preserve oneself" from the contamination of sexuality, came to be seen as the ideal expression of Christian faith. Dedicated following of the Gospel could take place only if one separated oneself from the temptations and involvements of the "world" and, at least symbolically but often in reality, went to the desert. When this was combined with the growing notion that sexuality was incompatible with the sacramental ministry, it was determined that ordained clergy should, even if married, abstain from all sexual activity. Therefore married life was denied full participation in Christian faith for it was neither clerical nor monastic. Marriage was second-best; the idea of "vocation" was appropriated to those Christians who were called to a "higher way of life."

Another major element in the development of Christians' understanding of marriage came during this same period with the migrations of Teutonic peoples into southern Europe. These groups brought with them their own customs, values, and laws which, as these invaders gradually intermingled with the local population, interacted with the outlook and practices of Christians in the Mediterranean area. Among these Teutonic peoples a strong emphasis on tribal identity and continuity brought back to center stage society's role in marriage. Contrary to accepting the couple's consent as the principal agent of a marriage—which was the Roman viewpoint—the Teutonic viewpoint laid stress on marriage as a contract verified by socially conventionalized arrangements.

In this northern European perspective the economic arrangements associated with marriage, the dowry and bridal gift, took on intrinsic importance as part of the contractual action. Obviously such arrangements were of concern to the families of the bride and groom, so they were not left just to the bridal couple. But the act of intercourse itself was seen as intrinsic to the enactment of a marriage, though only when linked with some agreement to marriage on the part of the two persons.

As from the ninth century onward Europe moved into the Middle Ages, there was increased involvement of society in the initiation and validation of marriage, increased emphasis on the contractual character of the couple's marital consent, and increased attention to first sexual intercourse as constitutive of the married state. It might be instructive to mention, however, that such formal understanding and practice was true of the upper classes much more than it was of the bulk of the population. For the typical peasant marriage was basically a "natural" happening that occurred quite informally and without benefit of social notice or regulation.

Educated Christians in the Middle Ages viewed marriage in the light of the inherited Patristic judgments, particularly St. Augustine's listing of the "goods" toward which marriage should be directed. Among these goods the *bonum prolis*—the "good of offspring"— enjoyed a certain primacy, for it was quite obviously the goal towards which the act of intercourse was biologically directed. It was clearly the divine intent for marriage, so it could justify a Christian experiencing the irrationality and passion, the carnal pleasure, and the sensual gratification of concupiscence that were intrinsic to sexual activity. Another good, the "good of the sacrament," was always recognized as having some superior value, but for the most part it was only vaguely understood.

What was happening as Europe began to reshape itself after the upheavals associated with the collapse of the Roman Empire and the Teutonic migrations south was an increasing emphasis on public recognition, including (as we will see) Church recognition, of the marriage contract. Married people were, then, those whose state of cohabitation conformed to these social agreements. Marriage existed not only in connection with such public, or at least publicly verifiable, acts but *because* of them. That particular "state in life" was caused by the couple's contractual consent and, to an extent about which there was differing opinion, by their actual sexual intercourse, but that consent had to be given in a manner that society recognized.

In the midst of this increased structuring of the marriage arrangement, there continued to be a grass roots recognition of a prior power of the two people to bring their marriage into existence. Despite the lesser regard in which they were held and negative judgments made upon them by both Church and state, common law marriages, in which a couple simply began to live together without recognition by either Church or state, remained a widespread reality. So widespread was the practice that Church and civil governments had no alternative but to give such unions a basic status as some kind of real marriage.

Since the sixteenth century and the reforms of the Council of Trent, Catholic understanding of marriage has been dominated by the teaching and practice of the Church. With the regulation that an official Church witness in the person of a duly empowered priest was needed for valid contracting of a marriage, common-law marriage lost what status it had, and the public marriage ceremony was seen to be that by which two people became married. Church law and in some instances civil law recognized "consummation" of the marriage contract by the couple's intercourse as "completing" the marriage arrangement. But in the minds of the people, Catholics included, two persons were married if by a fundamentally free choice and not hindered by some barrier such as being already married to someone else, they had gone through the required public actions, whether they be civil or religious.

For men and women in the modern Western world, it is the legal arrangements that essentially distinguish the married from the unmarried. While the inner attitude of the spouses towards one another has been valued, two people have not been seen to be married or not because of the presence or absence of marital love and concern. There are "happy" and "unhappy" marriages, but they are all marriages, unless the latter cease to exist because of the legal arrangement of divorce.

This is not to say that there has been no reflection by Catholics on the inner reality of marriage. Just the contrary. Like others in the West, Catholics have been deeply touched by the greater emphasis on romantic love that has marked modern understanding of marriage. Linked with the more general growth in appreciation for the basic dignity and autonomy of the individual human person, regardless of social status or race or sex or talent, this shift towards the personal aspects of the married couple's life together has, in the past half-century, triggered an important reassessment of Catholic views of marriage.

Coming into the twentieth century, Catholics thought about marriage in terms of the so-called "ends (or goals) of marriage," even though the ordinary Catholic knew nothing about the technical debates about these "ends." Actually the goals being discussed by moral theologians and Church authorities and being explained to the faithful in sermons and religious instruction were the three classic "goods" stated by St. Augustine with two important differences. First, for a variety of reasons, generation of children had assumed almost unchallenged primacy as the goal of marriage with the result that ethical explanation of marital responsibility focused lopsidedly on birth control. Second, the notion of sacrament was applied to marriage almost exclusively in reference to the wedding ceremony, which was a use of the word quite different from that of St. Augustine or of most of Christian history.

Shortly before mid-century doctrinal and theological concentration on procreation as the primary goal of Catholic marriage began to be openly challenged, and within a few years the human and Christian relation of the two people to one another achieved recognition as an equal, if not superior, purpose of marriage. This more personalistic view, which sees marriage as a free society of people and not primarily as an institution of nature (with emphasis on the biological level of humans as part of nature), received important support at the Second Vatican Council and has become a controlling force in present-day Catholic understanding of marriage.

What Is Distinctive About Christian Marriage?

Looking at the earliest centuries of Christianity, we might be tempted to say that there was nothing distinctive about Christian marriage, at least in the sphere of social arrangement and social identification. But that would be an oversimplification. While no specific Christian official action, such as a marriage liturgy, was thought to be needed for a Christian man and woman to marry, there were various forms of recognition by the Christian communities to which they belonged that gave their marriage approval, blessing, and social impact.

As early as the letters of Ignatius at the end of the first century, there is reference to the married couple receiving some approval and blessing from Church leadership. While there is no indication that such blessing was thought to be necessary to the marriage, it seems that Christians were expected to choose marriage within the context of Christian community life and in accord with the lifestyle of Christians. Still there was no Church wedding or specific role of the Church in bringing the marriage into existence. The Church recognized that a couple had married, celebrated that fact, and prayed for God's blessing on the union.

Gradually the blessing by the head of the community, bishop or presbyter, assumed greater prominence in people's view. While not required, the approval and blessing of the head of the community was seen as something that devout Christians should obtain, as an indication that they were truly marrying "in Christ."

But if the external formality of marriage among Christians in the early centuries was basically that of their particular cultural situation so that one finds no distinctively Christian marriage ceremony, the understanding of Christian marriage and consequently its conduct were distinctive. New Testament texts, for example the fifth chapter of Ephesians, indicate that Christians almost immediately linked the significance of their married relationship to the love between Christ and the Church. The term sacrament as we have used it in more recent centuries was not applied to marriage between two Christians, but the understanding that marriage was transformed in its meaning by the meaning of Christ's Passover—which is what we mean by saying that Christian marriage is a sacrament—goes back to the first Christian generation.

It is not clear just when and in what way the initiation of a Christian marriage was linked to a special celebration of the Eucharist. Probably the earliest form of this was simply a special reference to a couple's marriage, perhaps a special blessing, in the context of the regular community Eucharist. However, for more than a millenium there was no celebration of Eucharist that included as an early portion of the liturgy the actual marriage ceremony.

In Eastern Christianity the blessing given the marrying couple by the officiating priest or bishop came to be considered the cause of the marriage bond. This was not the case in the West. Even in the post-Tridentine discipline that requires the presence of a priest with proper authority, the priest is a witness, and his blessing just that. The two persons are themselves the effective agents of the marriage bond. Marriage is thought of as a contract, and they are the contracting parties. Still the common perception of Catholics has been that the priest's action married them, and Church authorities and Church law did not energetically contest this understanding.

The Middle Ages and early modern times saw an increasing intervention of the official Church in the initiation of a Christian marriage. This resulted in the view that a Christian marriage came into existence through the sacramental ceremony; to be a partner to a Christian marriage one had to be "married in the Church." For Catholics this view was crystallized in the decree *Tametsi* of the Council of Trent, which stated as the requirement for a valid marriage the presence of a duly empowered ordained minister in addition to two formal witnesses to the marriage contract.

Without this "proper form" no Catholic marriage came to be. With a ceremony containing the elements of this form an indissoluble bond was established. To some extent the absolute indissolubility of this bond was provisional, for Church law continued to recognize the possibility of dissolving a marriage that had been publicly formalized *(ratum)* but not yet consummated by the couple's first consequent act of sexual intercourse. Obviously for a Catholic marriage to be such, the content of the marital contract must be that proper to Christian marriage. In modern times the Catholic Church has seen the substance of this contract to be the mutual exchange of exclusive rights to sexual intercourse as directed to procreation. So clear was the emphasis on the procreational goal, the *bonum prolis*, that a marriage agreement between two people which excluded the generation of children could not be considered a true marriage contract.

In this context of emphasis on the legally established form and content of the marriage ceremony, what appeared to be distinctive of Catholic marriage was conformity in form and in the couple's intentions to the legal prescriptions. Those who had distinctively Catholic marriages were those who were "married in the Catholic Church." There was also, of course, an intrinsic difference; the bond established by a "Church marriage" enjoyed an indissolubility that did not characterize other human marriages, though other *Christian* marriages shared this indissolubility up to a point. Moreover both the distinctive character and indissolubility were rooted in the fact that Catholic marriages were "sacramental"; marriage was one of the seven sacraments of the Church and therefore a God-given cause of grace. This was reiterated as a regular element of Catholic teaching, but the meaning of the statement was seldom understood, which leads to our third topic.

What Is Meant by Calling Christian Marriage a Sacrament?

The third chapter in this volume will treat more analytically and at greater length the Catholic theology of marriage. However, some historical review of the evolution of this theology can be helpful in making it more understandable. That will be the purpose here.

Two words, the Latin word *sacramentum* and the Greek word *mysterion*, stand at the beginning of Christian use of the term sacrament. It is several centuries before *sacramentum* is used, and then not with the meaning we give it when calling marriage a sacrament. On the other hand, there is a much earlier connection with the word *mysterion*, even though its earliest use does not directly name the sacramentality of the relation between Christian spouses.

Probably the earliest verbal evidence is found in the epistle to the Ephesians. This is the well-known passage in the fifth chapter where Christ's relation to the Church is seen as the exemplar of the relation which should exist between Christian husband and wife.

Mysterion is used to characterize the revelation of God's saving self-giving that finds expression in Jesus' death and resurrection. Since the meaning of marriage is intertwined with this meaningful *mysterion* of Christ's death and resurrection, Christian marriages share in this mystery.

This passage in Ephesians indicates that marriage in general, and in a special way marriage between Christians, is a symbolic reality that reveals the divine saving love. Actually this early Christian view is grounded in the Israelitic prophets' use of human marriage as a metaphor to interpret the relation of Yahweh to Israel. From the time of Hosea onward, the image of Israel as the bride of Yahweh—often a wayward bride—figures prominently in the prophetic teaching, pointing both to Israel's repeated infidelity and to the unconditional faithfulness of Israel's God.

In the New Testament the Gospels and the Pauline epistles pick up this metaphor and give it a christological focus. Jesus is himself the bridegroom of the new covenant people. In his death and resurrection he has given himself to his bride, the Church, and history will be the process of preparing this bride for the final nuptials of unending life. Though it will have an uneven history of interpretation, this imagery of Christ/Church and husband/wife will continue as an element of Christian theology of the Church and its sacramentality.

This idealistic view of marriage as revelatory of God's love manifested in Jesus, plus the biblical insistence that God had created all things good, passed on to early Christianity a very positive view of human sexuality and marriage. However, in interaction with other ancient understandings of sexuality, the Fathers of the Church, as we saw, quickly incorporated into their explanation of marriage a disastrous negativity. Faced with the texts of Genesis, the Fathers had to recognize that God had created marriage, or at least some form of marriage, good. But the original sin of Adam and Eve had introduced evil into the picture, and marriage as it now exists, vitiated by sexual lust and irrationality, was the result. Procreation of children can provide some justification for marriage. Marriage can also serve to keep sexuality within certain bounds. But it does not take much reflection to realize that the Patristic tradition leaves little possibility that marital sexuality, rooted as it is in sin, can reflect the divine saving love.

Patristic thinking on marriage finds in St. Augustine of Hippo a synthetic expression that dominates centuries of subsequent Christian thought and practice. Though St. Augustine's view was not as negative as that of many of his Patristic predecessors nor in itself as negative as is often assumed, it is clearly controlled by his understanding of original sin. Interpreting the Genesis passage about Adam and Eve as a description of an actual historical occurrence, a gravely sinful action performed a few thousand years before by two historical personages, St. Augustine believed that a "wound" from this sin passed down through all of human history. While St. Augustine did not agree with the view that this original sin was precisely the act of sexual intercourse, he taught that from the original sin there resulted in humans an imbalance in erotic attraction and passionate response that inevitably debased human sexuality, even in marriage.

According to St. Augustine sexual expression is never without grave sin outside marriage; even within marriage it is always touched by venial sin unless the couple desire only the generation of a child and do not directly seek the pleasure attached to intercourse. Thus procreation and nurture of children is for St. Augustine the first and dominant "good" that Christians should seek in their marriage. A second "good" is personal fidelity upon which each can depend, and here there are indications that St. Augustine places positive value on friendship between husband and wife, though he does not develop this element in his description of a Christian marriage. The third "good" is the unbreakable bond in a Christian marriage, and it is this permanence of their marriage commitment which St. Augustine calls the *sacramentum*. Clearly this use of the term does not point directly to the deeper symbolic dimension of Christian marriage.

Yet in the strange logic of historical use of words, the word sacrament became part of the Christian explanation of marriage and acquired a changed meaning as sacrament itself took on new theological significance. For the most part medieval theologians concentrated in their explanations of marriage on the procreative function, on the role of contractual consent in establishing a marriage, and on marriage providing a "remedy" for the unruly sexual attractions that come with concupiscence. However, at least as early as the writings of Hugh of St. Victor in the twelfth century, we find explicit teaching about the symbolic role of the married relationship and its reflection of the relation between Christ and the Church or between God and the individual Christian. Since there was agreement that somehow Christian marriage constituted a situation of grace, a natural situation of friendship and support with the possibility of overcoming sexual temptations, the ingredients for describing Christian marriage as a sacrament of the Church were now in place.

However, several centuries would elapse before the sacramentality of Christian marriage would receive much attention. The reason for this was that the procreative purpose of marriage continued to be stressed as primary. Only in the midtwentieth century would the personal relatedness of wife and husband, that aspect of marriage which is capable of bearing metaphorical reference to the relation of God to humans, begin to receive acceptance as a primary purpose of Christian marriage.

Though this new insistence on marriage as primarily a community of persons relating to one another in love and Christian faith initially received opposition, its acceptance by the Second Vatican Council has opened up a new stage in Catholic appreciation of marriage as sacrament. Today our theology locates the distinctiveness of Christian marriage in the injection of the transforming significance of Jesus' death and resurrection into the relation between the spouses. Married love and life is transformed as a human experience because of its perceived role as a revelation of God's loving presence to humans. On this the following chapter expands.

Footnote

[1]Actually there is not much literature on the history of Christian marriage. Apart from incidental treatment in broader works on Western history or on the history of the Church, one can find little specific study of marriage as a Christian reality apart from the items listed in the bibliography attached to this essay. Probably the most helpful volume is that of T. Mackin, *What is Marriage?*

References

Mackin, Theodore, *What is Marriage?* New York: Paulist Press, 1982. A thorough study of the historical development of Catholic theology and jurisprudence of marriage from New Testament times to the present. Probably the best one-volume treatment of Christian marriage available.

Martos, Robert. *Doors to the Sacred.* Garden City, N.Y.: Doubleday, 1981. Contains a rather lengthy (pp. 397–452) review of the history of marriage in the Catholic Church with an emphasis on the question of indissolubility.

Schillebeeckx, Edward. *Marriage: Human Reality and Saving Mystery.* New York: Sheed & Ward, 1965. A pioneering study of the history and meaning of Christian marriage. Still a valuable source.

Stevenson, Kenneth. *Nuptial Blessing, A Study of Christian Marriage Rites.* Notre Dame, Ind.: Notre Dame University Press, 1983. An historical study of Christian marriage from a liturgical viewpoint, an indispensable tool for studying the history and theology of marriage.

3. THEOLOGY OF CHRISTIAN MARRIAGE

William Roberts

Christian theology is not meant to be a merely intellectual, academic exercise that stands aloof from life. It should instead flow from the faith experience of people and in turn enlighten and enrich that experience. In doing so it uses the insights and critical evaluations of other ways of knowing, particularly the social and behavioral sciences. This chapter is intended then to draw from and interact theologically with the social scientific understandings of marriage that are described in the Fischer/Hart chapter that opens this volume.

At the beginning of that chapter, the authors detailed the various elements of change that figure so largely in the experience of our contemporaries and that have a major impact on long-term institutions such as marriage. To live in today's world is to be constantly conscious of the impermanence of whatever now is and to be aware that there is no avoiding movement into a future that is unclear and risky. As that chapter pointed out, it is in this context that there is increasing emphasis on the fact that marriage is a *process* with distinctive possibility, problems, challenges, and patterns of development.

Christian Marriage as Eschatological Process

This model for thinking about marriage acquires theological enrichment through the central biblical outlook of eschatology. Eschatology points to the fact that human history is still on the way to its goal, is still unfulfilled and incomplete and somewhat sinful, and is being directed by God towards its final goal in ways that are often hidden or paradoxical.

For many centuries Christian theology spoke of the celibate state of life as being specially symbolic of the *eschaton*, the world to come where, as Jesus is reported to have said, "there is neither marrying nor giving in marriage." The underlying presumption of the claim that celibacy bore this eschatological significance was that it was a superior way of life, since it did not involve sexuality. As long as this negativity towards human sexuality prevailed, and marriage was seen as a "second-best" way of being Christian, the profoundly eschatological symbolism of marriage was obscured. However, with the recent recognition of the positive sacramentality of marriage, it is clear that Christian marriage is of its very nature eschatological.

All marriage, of course, points to the future, because it is from the sexual love of the couple that the future generation of humans comes. Beyond this obvious fact lies the futurity of all friendship and of the marital love of Christian spouses in a distinctive way. Entering into a friendship is itself a promise of future fidelity, and it is this fidelity that biblical authors since the time of Israel's prophets have used to symbolize human hope that God will fulfill the promise of salvation. Marital fidelity, encompassing much more than just sexual fidelity, makes divine fidelity believable; this is one of the key sacramentalities of marriage.

Furthermore there is a mysterious aspect of love which lovers experience: it is stronger than death. Unless there were something about personal friendship that could transcend death as a negation of the love, human friendship would be almost unbearably tragic, and it would be difficult to see how it could function to symbolize a loving God. Above all, when human love extends to loving God, as it is meant to do in Christian life, it would be a cruel deception if love did not somehow continue into life beyond physical death. So St. Paul can tell the early Christians of Corinth that, no matter what else passes away, love will carry on into unending life (1 Cor 13:9-12).

The comparison in Eph 5 between married love and Jesus' love for the Church confirms this eschatological character of married love, for it was in passing into risen life that Jesus became able to relate in saving love to all humans.

Intrinsic to the sacramental significance of Christian marriage is its promise of love's eschatological fulfillment in risen life. Apart from this marital symbolism Eucharist as a pledge of unending life and celibacy as a chosen form of Christian life could not have the eschatological meaning they have.

Eschatological does not apply to marriage only in terms of life after death; marriage, because it is a process, is inevitably directed to the future. The couple's love for one another along with their faith and love relationship to Christ is a development; an entire lifetime is spent in translating their Christian discipleship into their married life. Only gradually do the two persons express the sacrament which they are; only gradually does "the new creation" which they are as individuals and as a couple come into being.

The notion of dynamic process is implied also when the family is called a "domestic Church." The Church is a pilgrim people on a journey towards the fuller holiness and more complete union with God that will come only in the end time.[1] Both the family and the Church exist eschatologically, involved in a process of growth towards fulfillment in the world beyond. This is but another way of saying that a Christian couple, a Christian family, and the Church as a whole live out the mystery of Jesus' death and resurrection; they are always dying to what has been and moving into the new life of Christ's Spirit.

Christian Family Life as a Saving Sacrament, as Domestic Church

In studying marriage and family life as a process, social scientists have drawn attention also to the fact that this process involves a complex social situation within which individuals develop their personhood. It is worthwhile, then, to reflect theologically on this reality and to draw from the viewpoint of the Second Vatican Council in examining the way in which family life conditions the growth in holiness of its members. Unlike the First Vatican Council, which focused almost exclusively on the hierarchical structure of the Church, the Second Vatican Council emphasized the Church as the people of God. In their treatment of marriage and the family, the bishops of the council went on to apply the term "Church" to the family; the family is a domestic Church:

> From the wedlock of Christians there comes the family, in which new citizens of human society are born. By the grace of the Holy Spirit received in baptism these are made children of God, thus perpetuating the people of God through the centuries. The family is, so to speak, the domestic Church. In it parents should, by their word and example, be the first preachers of the faith to their children.[2]

To call the family a domestic Church is not simply to say that the family is a portion of the whole Church. Rather, it says that what is meant by Church is present and manifested in the family. The Christian family is a domestic Church because it is a community of believers who witness to their faith by sharing in worship and by sharing in Christ's ongoing redemptive mission.

First, the Christian family is a community of believers. Sociologically speaking the family is the basic unit of human society, grounded in the sexual expression of human love and blood relationship. To speak of the family as a community of faith is to stress the active sense of community; it is a sharing of commitment to, hope in, and love of Jesus Christ. It involves a shared endeavor to shape life according to the vision of the Gospel. The members of the family are meant to guide, inspire, and support each other in this pursuit. The choice of priorities in their life together and the decisions about shared activities or about the way in which individual activity is to fit into their common life are meant to be grounded in their shared Christian faith.

The true Christian family is Church, people of God, in which each finds strength from the others in pursuit of Christian holiness. On a small scale the Christian family is meant to be what the Church as a whole should be.

Second, the Christian family should share worship. Basically, of course, worship is an acknowledgement of the God who is revealed in Jesus. This acknowledgement takes in the whole of a person's perspective on life. It is an admission that God really is as Jesus described God to be, that this God is the source of life who raised Jesus to new life by the life-giving Spirit, and that this God is the transcendent reality beyond human imagining or thought who incredibly enters into familiar relationship with humans. To live in willing reverence of such a God and to accept being loved and saved by such a God are what it means to worship. So the entire life together of a family should be a practical everyday acknowledgement of this God.

While living this attitude is fundamental, we humans need to express it more explicitly, especially if we are to share it with one another. External acts of worship have always been intrinsic to human religion, and any group of Christians, like the family, has the need from time to time to state in some fashion its acceptance of the reality and ultimate importance of God. So on the most basic level the Christian family witnesses to the promise of Christ that when two or three gather together in his name, he is in their midst. With him present among them, the members of the Christian family can, in whatever way is genuine for them, give praise to God as "the Father of Our Lord Jesus Christ."

Worship is distinctive to Christians because they share by baptism in the priestly character and mission of Christ.

The baptized, by regeneration and the anointing of the Holy Spirit, are consecrated into a spiritual house and a holy priesthood. Thus through all those works befitting Christians they can offer spiritual sacrifices and proclaim the power of Him who has called them out of darkness into his marvelous light.[3]

Through prayer together members of a family express their union with each other in Christ and nourish that union. They do this when they share in family prayer at home and when as a family they participate in the worship of the larger parish community. These two situations of prayer are meant to complement one another. By sharing at home, people can become adept at more spontaneous prayer and at formulating their own prayer. They become more comfortable taking leadership roles in worship and in sharing what is most intimate and hence often difficult to speak about publicly: their personal relationship to Christ in faith. This can help prepare them to assume active roles in parish worship and to witness their individual and family faith in parish services.

On the other hand, participation in parish liturgy can help the family avoid isolation from the mainstream of Christian life. In the parish the members of the family should discover the broad Christian experience of others, be challenged by the proclamation and explanation of the Gospel, and become part of the parish's commitment to bettering the world. But it is also in the parish that a Christian family can more fully give sacramental witness to other families, witness that living out family life in the context of Christian faith can make sense and bring happiness. Through parish worship Christian families and the parish community are meant to support and enrich one another.

Third, the family is meant to share in the mission of Christ as he continues to save human history. This mission is one of proclaiming the Gospel and working to promote the kingdom of God. God's kingdom touches both present and future. Its full realization will come only beyond history in the end time, but it is already partially present in history and moving towards its final fulfillment. It is present in history insofar as humans strive to live in equal dignity and justice and peace and personal concern for one another. The Christian family is meant to nourish concern for the disadvantaged and oppressed, to help prepare members of the family for responsible sharing in the task of righting injustices, and when appropriate to participate as a family in public life.

The Second Vatican Council pointed Christians towards this broader reality of mission, recognizing the need for developing the internal faith and life of individuals and families, but urging them to reach out beyond their own parochial interests:

> The Council focuses its attention on the world, the whole human family along with the sum of those realities in the midst of which that family lives. It gazes upon that world which is the theater of human history, and carries the marks of human energies, triumphs, and tragedies; that world which the Christian sees as created and sustained by its Maker's love, fallen indeed into the bondage of sin, yet emancipated now by Christ.[4]

Members of families as individuals and the entire family as a corporate unit live out their Christian vocation by moving out beyond the family confines and sacramentalizing the healing presence of Christ to humankind. In his apostolic exhortation *On the Family*, Pope John Paul II suggests different levels at which a family can exercise this kind of ministry. One way is to address the social needs of others:

> Families therefore, either singly or in association, can and should devote themselves to manifold social service activities, especially in favor of the poor or at any rate for the benefit of all people and situations that cannot be reached by the public authorities' welfare organization.[5]

Beyond this the family has a contribution to make towards the creation of a new international order:

> In view of the worldwide dimension of various social questions, the family has seen its role with regard to the development of society extended in a completely new way: It now involves cooperating for a new international order, since it is only in worldwide solidarity that the enormous and dramatic issues of world justice, the freedom and the peace of humanity can be dealt with and solved.
>
> The spiritual communion between Christian families, rooted in a common faith and hope and given life by love, constitutes an inner energy that generates, spreads and develops justice, reconciliation, fraternity and peace among human beings. Insofar as it is a "small-scale church," it is meant to be a sign of unity for the world and in this way to exercise its prophetic role by bearing witness to the kingdom and peace of Christ, towards which the world is journeying.[6]

This mission of the family clearly applies to three critical areas in today's world: world peace, hunger, and human oppression. The entire planet lives under the shadow of threatened nuclear holocaust. This danger is not only a matter of international politics; it is the most compelling moral issue facing humans today. Christian families can contribute to peacemaking in a variety of ways. As a microcosm of human society, the family should work towards peace within itself; the larger society can scarcely become more peaceful than the units within it. But the family must also work for peace by becoming educated to the issues and by contributing to peace efforts through its shared talent, concern, and support.

In the matter of world hunger, the family members must look beyond their primary responsibility of providing food for one another and break bread with the needy in their neighborhood or parish or city. Today, where the causes and remedies of poverty are international in character, Christian families are challenged to involvement with the national and international movements aimed at confronting the scandal of widespread human starvation.

Finally Christian families must develop practical concern for the violation of people's rights in so many portions of the globe. Such concern must be rooted in family members' respect for each other's rights and freedom. However, as with world poverty the family must reach out to become part of the broad effort to overcome oppression.

Mission and worship are inseparable. Because the God revealed in Jesus is a God with special interest in "the little ones" of the earth, the poor, oppressed, and disadvantaged, Christians cannot genuinely acknowledge this God and at the same time ignore the needs of the marginal groups of society. Becoming part of the effort to better the life situation of the exploited poor is intrinsic to a Christian family's worship of God.

Marriage Is an Intimate Partnership of Life and Love Between Two Equal Persons, a Woman and a Man

There are two important parts to this statement. Each deserves to be considered in turn. Each can be understood more adequately because of the research and insights of the social sciences which the Fischer/Hart chapter summarized.

EQUALITY OF HUSBAND AND WIFE

Fischer and Hart detailed the cultural revolution taking place today with respect to the relationship between men and women and their respective roles in society. As they indicated, this is leading to a new perspective on marriage: the traditional view of the man being the source of authority and the one engaged in public affairs, while the woman is to take care of the home and the children and remain basically subordinate to her husband is no longer being accepted. Instead, marriage is being understood as a partnership of equals; the individuality of the partners, their personal relationship to one another, and their shared responsibility for all the elements of family life are being stressed.

Christian understandings of marriage have been touched by this social revolution. For centuries, Christians simply accepted the prevailing context of male dominance and the underlying presupposition of male superiority. Church as well as civic structures were developed on this false assumption that women were incapable of handling significant public tasks or of exercising leadership. In the Church this view was supported by the belief that this situation was not only divinely approved but actually rooted in the way that God had created men and women.

This gender prejudice was reflected in marriage. Wives were perceived as belonging to their husbands. A father gave his daughter away to her new male superior, her husband. Even in those cultures where the notion of the husband owning the wife had disappeared, the image of the husband as "head of the house" remained strong. Presumably this arrangement could be grounded in Christian teaching, and Scripture texts were (and still are) employed—with less than accurate exegesis—to give it religious legitimation.

What is needed, then, is a deepened theological understanding of the equality of men and women and of the relationship between them.

Christian theology in general, and specifically in the matter of the basic equality of human persons, can draw from religious insights of Israel that antedate Christianity by several centuries. Israelite religion, which meant the entirety of Israelite life, was governed by the notion of covenant, an alliance between the people and God. Implied in this was the social covenant among the people themselves, one in which each Israelite found identity and dignity because he or she pertained to this chosen people. Though expressed in the Law which God had given to Moses at Sinai, this fundamental dignity and personal worth of each Israelite was often overlooked in practice, so the great prophets of Israel consistently condemned the power brokers of Israelite society for neglecting the marginal elements, "the widow and the orphan."

There was not, however, a situation of complete personal equality in the Israel of Old Testament times. While they enjoyed a greater respect and better treatment than in many other ancient cultures, women were not in the full sense regarded as part of the chosen people. "Israel" was the men; a woman was part of the people only in terms of the particular man—father, husband, or son—in whose household she functioned. Respect and protection she might have, but not genuine equality. An indication of this unequal status was the fact that a woman was considered incapable of understanding the Law and therefore was not to be instructed in it, which of course made women subject to men's interpretation of the Law.

Yet there were some elements of theological insight that pointed towards recognition of women's equality. In the famous passage of Gen 2–3, which tells the story of human origins, the purpose of the text is not, as is so often supposed, to teach the subordination of women to men: man was created first; woman was derived from and therefore dependent upon him; woman was weaker and so succumbed to temptation and led man astray. Careful examination of the text suggests a much different reading.[7]

Basically the text is a theological statement that God is the author of human life and human marriage. While other animals are not equal to man and hence cannot be suitable partners, woman is bone of his bone and flesh of his flesh. For the ancient Hebrew bone and flesh referred to the total person. So the text is stating that woman is a person equal to man; as an equal she is a suitable partner. "That is why a man leaves his father and mother and clings to his wife, and the two of them become one body" (Gen 2:24).[8]

Significantly the familial authority of man over woman to which the text refers is not described as originally intended by God. Instead, both the suffering involved in childbirth and the actual social subordination of women are seen in the text to be the result of sin, not therefore intrinsically good or appropriate. Over the centuries this passage from Genesis, contrary to the inspired intent of its authorship, has been misused to legitimate the assignment of women to secondary status in human society.

Despite some progress towards acknowledging equality of women and men, the Judaism inherited by Jesus and earliest Christianity was a thoroughly patriarchal society in which male domination was simply taken for granted. Given that context, we are only now beginning to appreciate the break that occurred, at least briefly, with the inception of Christianity. Recent New Testament scholarship, for example Elisabeth Schüssler Fiorenza's *In Memory of Her,*[9] has reminded us that the attitude and behavior of Jesus towards women was a social revolution and a religious scandal. In the immediate post-Easter period many of Jesus' closest disciples were aware of this, with the result that the New Testament writings retain the tradition of Jesus dealing openly and publicly with women as equal persons, counting women among his disciples, even on occasion instructing them in the New Law. Women enjoyed unprecedented equality and responsibility in the early Christian communities; some were in primary leadership roles. No doubt elements of patriarchal attitude still affected these early Christian groups, but the governing theological principle was clearly and explicitly stated by Paul in Gal 3:28: in the Church there was to be no distinction made on ethnic, social, or sexual bases—"neither Jew nor Greek, slave nor free, male nor female."

One of the texts that indicates the extent to which the patriarchal cultural patterns of the Mediterranean world were mixed with the new Christian view of personal equality is in Eph 5:

> Be subject to one another out of reverence for Christ. Wives, be subject to your husbands, as to the Lord; for the man is the head of the woman, just as Christ is also the head of the Church. Christ is indeed, the savior of the body; but just as the Church is subject to Christ, so must women be to their husbands in everything.
>
> Husbands, love your wives, as Christ also loved the Church and gave himself up for it, to consecrate it, cleansing it by water and word, so that he might present the Church to himself all glorious. . . . In the same way men are bound to love their wives, as they love their own bodies. In loving his wife a man loves himself (Eph 5:21-28).

Because this text has been *the* classic reference for interpreting the respective roles of husband and wife in Christian marriage and has been for centuries enshrined in the wedding liturgy, it is essential to examine it carefully.[10]

The portion of the epistle in which this text is found is a detailing of the responsibilities of various members of the family; it closely resembles listings of household duties that had been circulated in that part of the world for at least the previous four centuries, listings that reflected the male-dominated structure of marriage. In a fashion similar to his handling of the issue of slavery in chapter six, the Pauline author does not challenge the social structure of marriage as he found it, nor does he give it his approval; it is simply there. His point is to insist that the relationships involved, especially that between husband and wife, be lived in an entirely new way, that is, in the spirit of Christ.

Actually the culturally accepted submission of wife to husband was qualified in a revolutionary way. First, the directive to wives and husbands is preceded by the general exhortation, "Be subject to one another out of reverence for Christ" (Eph 5:21). The deference then should be mutual and not one-sided. Second, the wife's response to the husband is in the context that he love her "as Christ loved the Church and gave himself up for her." His authority is that of love and not of domination; she is to respond to a lover's self-gift rather than to a master's command. Despite the patriarchal ring to Eph 5, its exhortation to live married life in the spirit of Christ implies a radical equality between the two persons that is incompatible with patriarchal attitudes. The text as it actually exists within the body of New Testament writing cannot be used—as it has so frequently been used—to justify the domination of wives by husbands as something intended by God or intrinsic to the reality of Christian marriage.

INTIMATE PARTNERSHIP

The preceding chapter describes the major shift in the understanding of and attitudes towards human sexuality that has marked the past few decades. While those elements of the so-called "sexual revolution" that touch upon extramarital sexual activity have received much more public attention, the more important development has probably come in terms of the changes within marriage. Deepened understanding of the personal dimension of human sexuality and a more positive appreciation of its contribution to people's psychological growth and balance have led to situating sexuality within the broader reality of friendship. Human intimacy is a goal broader and more basic than sexual intimacy; authentic sexual activity is but one contributor—though a most important contributor—to union between persons.

This sociopsychological insight has paralleled and probably subtly interacted with a development in Christian theological understanding of marriage. Grounded in the rediscovery of New Testament teaching about the basic equality of women and men in marriage as well as in other contexts of human life, contemporary Catholic teaching about marriage treats it as an intimate partnership of life and love. This is reflected, for example, in the Second Vatican Council's pastoral constitution, *Gaudium et spes*.[11] To

Christians over the centuries who have experienced their marriage to be such a partnership, this is no news. Seen, however, against the long history of the juridical view of marriage in official Roman Catholic circles, the teaching of the Second Vatican Council is quite revolutionary.[12]

The juridical approach is manifest in the 1918 Code of Canon Law, where marriage is referred to as a contract, and matrimonial consent is described as "an act of the will by which each party gives and accepts a perpetual and exclusive right over the body, for acts which are of themselves suitable for the generation of children."[13] In such a narrow focus on marriage, the proper consent and the ability to perform physically the act of sexual intercourse emerge as the essential constituent elements. Such a view considers love, personal intimacy, and deeper levels of sharing one's being with a spouse welcome additions to the marriage, but by no means essential.

In contrast to this, present-day advances in psychological understanding of marriage are marked, as we saw, by increased appreciation of the human, personal aspects of the relationship. Even prior to the Second Vatican Council, this had begun to influence Catholic moral theology's discussion of "the ends of marriage." Emphasis began to shift away from procreation and towards the mutual personal development of the two persons as the primary objective of marriage. With the Second Vatican Council conjugal love receives recognition as an indispensable component of authentic married life.

> This love is an eminently human one since it is directed from one person to another through an affection of the will. It involves the good of the whole person. Therefore it can enrich the expression of body and mind with a unique dignity, ennobling these expressions as special ingredients and signs of the friendship distinctive of marriage. . . .
> This love is uniquely expressed and perfected through the marital act. The actions within marriage by which the couple are united immediately and chastely are noble and worthy ones. Expressed in a manner which is truly human, these actions signify and promote that mutual self-giving by which spouses enrich each other with a joyful and thankful will.[14]

The description of marriage in the revised Code of Canon Law reflects the influence of the council's outlook.

> The marriage covenant, by which a man and a woman establish between themselves a partnership of their whole life, and which of its very own nature is ordered to the well-being of the spouses and to

the procreation and upbringing of children, has between the baptized been raised by Christ the Lord to the dignity of a sacrament.[15]

The personalist outlook of the Second Vatican Council is reflected also in the revised Code's description of marital consent. This consent is "an act of the will by which a man and a woman by an irrevocable covenant mutually give and accept one another for the purpose of establishing a marriage."[16] In his commentary on this passage,[17] Theodore Mackin points out the possible significance of the use of the Latin *tradunt* rather than *donant* for giving. The former word carries the meaning of self-surrender, of a giving over of self for the sake of another. In the Latin version of the New Testament, it is what Christ did for those he loved: "Tradidit semetipsum" (Gal 2:20).

In embracing more person-centered understandings of marriage, the Council did not elaborate an accompanying theology; it pointed only implicitly to such and left its development to postconciliar reflection. So far little has been done to describe the *theological* dimension of Christian married partnership, but we can suggest some of its elements. With marriage a shared life, a shared identity, a shared purpose and destiny come into existence. For a Christian married couple this means a new and shared identity as Christians grounded in the experience of *shared discipleship*. Married life together is not only a matter of mutual psychological maturation; it is a process of *shared growth in grace*, that is, an expansion of their human potential and personhood under the impact of God's self-giving. The purpose of married life is meant to be (as we will see in greater detail) a special *shared participation in the saving mystery of Jesus' death and resurrection*. Human sexuality as expressing the love of Christian woman and man cannot be described demeaningly as a "remedy for concupiscence" nor regarded as something "less good"; instead, it is a word that speaks about God as the supreme lover, a symbol revealing the depth of Christ's desire to give himself in friendship to humans, a uniquely uniting force that enters intrinsically into the divine action of bringing a new humanity into being.

Christian Marriage as a Sacrament

Modern research in the social and behavioral sciences has drawn attention to the elements of *meaning* and *presence* in marriage. What it means for a couple to be wife and husband and the extent to which they are truly for one another, present personally to one another, are of basic importance to the vitality and durability of the relationship. It is here that Christian faith with its insight into the *sacramentality* of marriage can qualitatively enrich the experience of married life, because sacramentality has to do precisely with meaning and presence.

While Catholic teaching has spoken for centuries of marriage as a sacrament, there has been relatively little clarification of what this designation involved, except that people had some belief that with the wedding ceremony the couple received somehow the strength needed to live out their relationship responsibly and faithfully. For Catholics marriage was one of the seven sacraments and therefore a "channel of grace."

For a variety of reasons, the idea of sacrament and the understanding of how sacraments affect people are at the present time undergoing important change. Instead of exclusive attention to the liturgical actions which we had come to identify as "the sacraments," we now realize that Christian sacraments reach out beyond these liturgical moments to embrace the entire context of people's lives.[18] All a Christian's existence is meant to be significant and indicates the saving presence of the risen Christ and his Spirit, which is what we mean by sacrament. Obviously such a change would have basic impact on what is meant by calling Christian marriage a sacrament.

Insight into the sacramentality of Christian marriage rests on two prior understandings: of Christ as sacrament of God and of the Church as sacrament of Christ. Sacraments are sensible signs through which God's self-gift is communicated to us and through which we can relate more intimately to God. Jesus of Nazareth is the human embodiment of God's self-revealing Word. It is through this human, Jesus, that who God is and what God is for us are most clearly and fully revealed. Because Jesus is human, sharing the basic experiences common to all of us, we can grasp this word about the reality of God "that surpasses all understanding."

Even though Jesus is no longer visibly present in history, Christians believe that he continues to exist in their midst as the risen Lord, continues to function as God's self-revealing Word, and shares with the faithful his own Spirit by which (as Paul mentions in Gal 4:6) they are able to relate to God as "Abba, Father." As Edward Schillebeeckx made clear in his pioneering book on the topic, Christ is the sacrament of our encounter with God.[19]

However, precisely because the risen Christ can no longer function as a sensible sign of divine presence, the Christian community, the Church, is needed in history as a sacrament of Christ. The primary mission of the Church is to proclaim by word and discipleship that Jesus is Christ and Lord and to promote in sensible ways the reign of God in human lives. As the Church—the community of the baptized—lives out this mission, and to the degree that it does so, it is a visible sign and effective agent of the invisible saving presence of the risen Christ and his Spirit. The Christian community is then by its entire existence the sacrament of Christ; everything that it is and does, with a special symbolizing role for its liturgical activity, is sacrament.

Within this global sacramentality of Christian life, married couples and their families are meant to play a distinctive sacramental role. Through the manifested saving effect of their love for one another, they are meant to witness to the ultimate saving power of God's loving presence to humans in history. While the wedding ceremony plays an important role in the sacramentality of this relationship, it cannot lay claim to being by itself the sacrament of Christian marriage; it is but one element in a much richer and more extensive reality. The sacrament of Christian marriage is the couple in their continuing gift of self to one another.

Two Christians prior to their marriage are by their baptism members of the Church; by their faith and discipleship they share in sacramentalizing Christ's presence. With their marriage they create a special shared faith and discipleship which bears sacramental witness in a new way. Within the Christian community, by the permanent and exclusive gift of self to one another that is symbolized in their marital intercourse, they reveal the nature of God's saving activity. This transforming, that is, saving, revelation touches them first of all. Their love and following of Christ inspires and nourishes the growth of their love for one another, and it guides the way they treat one another. At the same time the profoundly intimate and personally enriching experience of their love for one another enables them to grasp more realistically the loving gift of self of the risen Christ. Each in loving the other is meant to become aware of Christ's love for that other; each in being loved by the other is meant to experience being loved by Christ.

If this is what is meant by the sacramentality of Christian marriage, it clearly is something that cannot function automatically. Whether or not and to what degree a Christian couple experiences marriage as a sacrament of Christ's love depends on several factors. What meaning does being baptized Christians have for the couple and how do they allow that to influence the way they live? Who is Christ for them and to what degree do they experience Christ as a friend and as an important part of their lives? To what extent are they able to share their faith in Christ with one another? What is the quality of their love and relationship with each other? How intimate and communicative are they with one another in the totality of their lives as the years pass? To what degree do they manifest towards each other the respect, caring, self-giving, and passionate love that Christ has for his fellow humans?

When we say that Christian marriage is a sacrament, we are claiming that it, like the other sacraments of the Church, is a participation in the death and resurrection of Christ and a means by which the saving power of this death and resurrection touches and transforms people's lives.

Salvation implies that humans are liberated from evil, specifically from the root evil of sin. But this does not mean that God's saving action is one of taking away something called sin; rather, it is God's act of putting again into human lives that of which sin is the absence, the personal love by which humans come to maturity and happiness. Salvation is friendship and union with God manifested, experienced, and achieved in friendship and union with our fellow humans. To grow in the lifelong process of "being saved" is to develop as persons in our ability to accept the challenge involved in entering into authentic, mature relationships with God and with one another. To experience the salvation of Christ is to live, as Christ, in faith, trust, and a love that gives life to others. To live this way is the opposite of sin, which is alienation from God and from one another. It is by making possible for us a new relationship to God and to our fellow humans that Christ has saved us. Actual salvation, however, requires on the part of each person a genuine conversion of heart and mind.

Marriage is meant to be a distinctive way in which Christians can experience Christ's saving power. Growth together as a couple involves a lifelong maturing in faith and trust, in love and self-giving, a maturing that is rooted in their shared commitment to Jesus as the Christ. And such a shared growth, in which the personhood of each is redemptively transformed, takes place because of the experienced saving presence of Christ.

The Christ who is present to them is, however, the risen crucified one, and for a Christian to identify personally with him means the acceptance of the "entering into" the mystery of his death and resurrection. Each Christian begins this entry, this initiation, into Christ with her or his baptism, but the process of initiation is meant to continue throughout a person's life. Essentially this means that one has to let go of or die to whatever is a barrier to sharing in the new life of resurrection. It means moving from the darkness of sin to the light which is Christ; it means refusing the spirit of the world so that one can live by the Spirit of Christ; it means letting go of the past and accepting the change that is the price of moving into the future. Paul in his letter to the Christians of Rome puts this teaching in a graphic way:

> This we know: our old self was crucified with him so that the sinful body might be destroyed and we might be slaves to sin no longer. A man who is dead has been freed from sin. If we have died with Christ, we believe that we are also to live with him. We know that Christ, once raised from the dead, will never die again; death has no more power over him. His death was death to sin once for all; his life is life for God. In the same way you must consider yourselves dead to sin but alive for God in Christ Jesus (Rom 6:6–11).

Christian marriage is a way of life in which a couple lives out their relationship inspired by the sacrificial, that is, self-giving, love of the Christ who entered into new life by the complete gift of himself in death. This journey through life is made up of countless dyings and risings. Each must die to self-centeredness, jealousies, and petty bickerings in order to live in love and peace. Each must die to protective aloofness and the security of defensive distance in order to discover the new life of intimacy. Christians must die to their own narrow vested interests in order to become more fully gift for one another. Through such dyings and risings they grow increasingly into the risen Christ who continues to proclaim through them as sacrament, "This is my body given for you. Do this as remembrance of me." By such a life together the Christian couple are an eschatological sign. They point to that final achievement of love and new life which will take place when physical death itself will have given way to full sharing in Christ's risen existence.

Footnotes

1. See Second Vatican Council, *Lumen gentium* ch. 7. Text in Walter Abbot, ed., *The Documents of Vatican II* (New York: Guild Press, 1966).

2. *Lumen gentium* ch. 11.

3. *Lumen gentium* ch. 10.

4. Second Vatican Council, *Gaudium et spes* ch. 2.

5. Pope John Paul II, *Familiaris Consortio* (trans. from United States Catholic Conference, 1981) 44.

6. *Ibid.* 48.

7. See Edward Schillebeeckx, *Marriage: Human Reality and Saving Mystery* (New York: Sheed & Ward, 1965) 11-25.

8. For fuller treatment of this text, see William Roberts, *Marriage: Sacrament of Hope and Challenge* (Cincinnati: St. Anthony Messenger Press, 1983) 6-17.

9. E. Schüssler Fiorenza, *In Memory of Her* (New York: Crossroads, 1983) 68-159.

10. For a detailed exegesis of Eph 5:21-33, see Markus Barth, *Ephesians*, Anchor Bible, vol. 34A (Garden City, N.Y.: Doubleday, 1974) 607-753. A briefer exegesis can be found in T. Mackin, *What Is Marriage?* (New York: Paulist Press, 1982) 61-66; E. Schillebeeckx, *Marriage* 110-119; and W. Roberts, *Marriage* 29-37.

11. *Gaudium et spes* ch. 48.

12. The council's teaching on marriage is contained in *Gaudium et spes* chs. 47-52.

13. Canon 1081, 2.

14. *Gaudium et spes* ch. 49.

15. *The Code of Canon Law*, trans. by the Canon Law Society of Great Britain and Ireland (London: Collins Liturgical Publications, 1983) Canon 1055, 1.

16. Canon 1057, 2.

17. T. Mackin, *What Is Marriage?* 293.

18. See Bernard Cooke, *Sacraments and Sacramentality* (Mystic, Conn.: Twenty-third Publications, 1983).

19. Edward Schillebeeckx, *Christ the Sacrament of Our Encounter with God* (New York: Sheed & Ward, 1963).

References

Abbot, Walter M., general ed. *The Documents of Vatican II*. New York: Guild Press, 1966. The bishops' teaching on marriage is found in *Gaudium et spes* chs. 47-52.

Anzia, Joan Meyer, and Durbin, Mary G. *Marital Intimacy: A Catholic Perspective*. New York: Andrews and McMeel, Inc., 1980. This book resulted from a two-year colloquium between social scientists and theologians.

Capon, Robert Farrar. *Bed and Board: Plain Talk About Marriage*. New York: Simon and Schuster, 1965. Despite a certain datedness and some chauvinistic overtones, this book contains a number of good theological and practical insights into marriage from the perspective of a married Episcopal priest and theologian. The emphasis on the family meal is particularly good.

Cooke, Bernard. *Christian Sacraments and Christian Personality*. New York: Holt, Rinehart & Winston, 1965. The section on marriage (pp. 96-103) probes some of the important theological aspects of this sacrament.

Cooke, Bernard. *Sacraments and Sacramentality.* Mystic, Conn.: Twenty-third Publications, 1983. This book contains an excellent, updated treatment of the meaning of marriage in chapter 7.

Demuth, Paul E., ed. *Christian Marriage: Contract and Sacrament in Historical Focus.* St. Meinrad, Ind.: St. Meinrad School of Theology, 1967. This volume is the spring 1967 issue of *Resonance,* which was entirely dedicated to scholarly essays on canonical and theological aspects of marriage.

Dufresne, Edward R. *Partnership: Marriage and the Committed Life.* New York: Paulist Press, 1975. A balanced Christian reflection on marriage. Especially good is the author's treatment of solitude, sexual partnership, and time and possessions in marriage.

Dyer, George, ed. *Ministering to Marriage.* Mundelein, Ill.: Chicago Studies, 1979. This fall 1979 issue of *Chicago Studies* is totally comprised of essays on the history and theology of Christian marriage and on ministry to the engaged, to marital growth, and to marital failure.

Foley, Leonard, *Signs of Love: The Sacraments of Christ.* Cincinnati: St. Anthony Messenger Press. The chapter on marriage (pp. 85-95) presents on a very popular level some key theological insights.

Hart, Thomas N. *Living Happily Ever After: Toward a Theology of Christian Marriage.* New York: Paulist Press, 1979. This readable volume situates an understanding of marriage in the context of major contemporary theological themes. The author's theological insights regarding sex (ch. 5) are particularly helpful.

Hellwig, Monika. *The Meaning of the Sacraments.* Dayton, Ohio: Pflaum/ Standard, 1972. Chapter 6 studies the covenant dimension of marriage.

John Paul II. *On the Family (Familiaris Consortio).* Washington: U.S.C.C., 1982. This Apostolic Exhortation of December 15, 1981, emerged from the Synod of Bishops in the autumn of 1980.

Kasper, Walter. *Theology of Christian Marriage.* Minneapolis: Seabury Press, 1980. This is a technical study of marriage intended for scholars and ecclesiastics.

Kerns, Joseph. *The Theology of Marriage.* New York: Sheed & Ward, 1964. This volume amounts to an anthology of theological statements on marriage and sexuality through the centuries.

Massachusetts Commission on Christian Unity. *Ecumenical and Pastoral Directives on Christian Marriage.* Needham Heights, Mass.: Whittemore Associates, Inc. This booklet, published in the early 1970's, contains unofficial statements about marriage from the Roman Catholic, Eastern Orthodox, and representative Protestant perspectives.

Richards, Hubert, and DeRosa, Peter. *Christ in Our World.* Milwaukee: Bruce, 1966. In chapter 8 Richards treats of marriage in light of Scripture. In chapter 9 DeRosa relates marriage to life in the contemporary world.

Roberts, William P. *Marriage: Sacrament of Hope and Challenge.* Cincinnati: St. Anthony Messenger Press, 1983. This volume, written for a general readership, reflects on Christian marriage as a sacrament of the love between Christ and his Church and points to the practical implications that this theological insight has for experiencing a happier and more satisfying married life.

Silbermann, Eileen Zieget. *The Savage Sacrament: A Theology of Marriage after American Feminism.* Mystic, Conn.: Twenty-third Publications, 1983. Despite its tendency toward overkill, this volume makes a contribution in providing a feminist critique of a male-dominated theology and jurisprudence of marriage in the Roman Catholic Church.

Taylor, Michael J., ed. *The Sacraments: Readings in Contemporary Sacramental Theology.* New York: Alba House, 1981. This book includes two reprinted essays (pp. 183–203) dealing with a historical and theological perspective of marriage.

Whitehead, Evelyn Eaton, and James D. *Marrying Well: Possibilities in Christian Marriage Today.* Garden City, N.Y.: Doubleday, 1981. In this lengthy volume the authors bring together their combined theological and psychological expertise to probe significant dimensions of contemporary Christian marriage.

RITUALS

PRACTICAL LITURGICAL SUGGESTIONS FOR A WEDDING CELEBRATION AND FOR FAMILY LITURGIES: *THE WEDDING CELEBRATION*

Kathleen Fischer and Thomas Hart

Even if joined to the celebration of the Eucharist, the liturgical ritual of the wedding celebration should be clearly seen as a distinct sacramental rite. As such it need not require celebration of the Eucharist, though circumstances might indicate that this is appropriate. For example, if most of those gathered for the wedding understand the intrinsic link between marriage and Eucharist, sharing in the Eucharist would be seen as a distinctive celebration of the new marriage.

The wedding ritual should make clear that the ministers of the sacrament are the married couple. Theirs, then, should be the key role and central spatial position. In the midst of the assembled community, they should witness to and celebrate their shared Christian faith and new joint discipleship, that is, they should be sacrament.

On the other hand, the liturgical activity of the ordained minister should reflect his role in the celebration, that of a witness representing the parish community and beyond that the larger community of the Church. This follows from our theology of the Church, but, as our earlier chapters indicated, it is also suggested by the need married couples have to see themselves "located" in the larger context of society.

As a representative of the Church's theological understanding of marriage, the ordained minister can appropriately give a homily on the texts selected by the couple, but it would also be in place for this to be joined to a shared reaction to the texts by the assembled community, particularly by those who are married couples. Again, but clearly in the role as representative of the Church, the minister can assure the couple of the support of this larger community and in its name bless them. If the wedding is celebrated in conjunction with the Eucharist, the homily should link the intrinsic sacramentalities of Christian marriage with those of the Eucharist, making clear that this particular Eucharist is part of the *celebration* of the wedding.

Given the present-day acknowledgement of the personal equality of women and men, the patriarchal ceremony of the father giving the bride away should be dropped. Instead, there could be some symbolic action of the bride and the groom giving her or his family to the other as part of the self-giving that is the central symbolism of the wedding. This could be joined to a symbolic act of each family giving its son/daughter to his or her new spouse. The appropriateness of these two actions would depend upon such things as the extent to which the bride and groom are still in close contact with their families, whether there is a context of extended family of which they will become a part, or whether the parents of one or the other are divorced.

Along with this family involvement, or in some cases instead of it, intimate friends, because of their formative influence and continuing interaction with the new couple, could be part of the originating and supportive circles recognized in the ritual. In this way the ritual will make clear that the new marriage community, though essentially the husband and wife, is meant to extend beyond them.

Some ritual action should manifest the assembled community's pledge of support for the newly married couple. Social studies have made abundantly clear the need for a couple to experience such support. This might be an occasion for the priest who is acting as official Church witness to add a pledge of the entire Church's support. Along with such a pledge the people, or some representatives acting in their name, and the official witness could give their blessing to the couple by some gesture such as placing their hands on the heads of the kneeling groom and bride. Or with a short explanation this might be linked to the giving of the kiss of peace.

If the Eucharist follows, the couple should be given the opportunity to explain to the community that they see this as celebrating the sacrament they now are, a celebration that they hope will continue in their Eucharistic participation over the years. They might invite their assembled friends to see the Eucharist as beginning the celebration that will carry on into the wedding reception and festivities.

The liturgy should carefully avoid any sexist language or any suggestion of a subordination of the woman to the man. In particular the wedding vows should make clear the equality of the two persons and the individual freedom with which they commit themselves to creating a shared life.

A wedding is a rite of passage. A Christian marriage reinterprets this passage by incorporating the meaning of Jesus' passage through death into the new life of resurrection. The wedding liturgy must make clear the way in which Christian marriage finds its deepest meaning in terms of this death/new life mystery. So an essential element of the liturgy must be a highlighting of the risen Lord's *presence* to the assembled community, a presence which the new couple begins to sacramentalize in a distinctive way.

As shared Christian life and shared Christian identity, marriage is also meant to be shared Christian ministry and discipleship. The wedding liturgy should provide some occasion for the couple to assume responsibility for participating in the Church's mission, pledging support to one another in each one's individual ministry and mature cooperation in shared ministerial activities. To help achieve this, the theme of the kingdom of God could appropriately be introduced into the liturgy, permitting not only the couple but all those present to commit themselves to working for realization of the kingdom.

The wedding ritual should explicitly refer to Christian marriage as a personal communion in love and intimacy which then extends in mature generativity to creation of a family as a lovingly open and concerned union of persons. This could be done in conjunction with the couple praying for the personal qualities that will be required to bring about such a mature relationship and through the assembled community joining them in this prayer. In particular the sacramentalism of Christian marriage as revealing Christ's loving and life-creating self-gift in resurrection should be stressed in the homily. At the same time the liturgy should call attention to the essential link between following Jesus and being concerned with the needs of one's sisters and brothers; it should challenge the couple to think of their love as having broader scope than merely one another, and their generativity as extending beyond biological children.

Married couples need good preparation and ongoing support

if their marriages are to succeed. The first chapter in this volume should make that clear. Consequently the importance of the surrounding community as support system to the new couple deserves emphasis in the nuptial celebration.

The wedding liturgy would do well to use metaphors of journey and growth rather than those of structure and institution, to make clear that marriage is a continuing process. Scripture with its symbolism of exodus and its parables of growth is a valuable liturgical resource.

Practical Liturgical Suggestions: Family Structures

Family prayer should reflect the equality of husband and wife; they should function as coleaders of family prayer and should cooperatively shape family liturgies. Together they should inspire and guide the growing participation of children, not just confining them to the parents' own familiar expressions of faith but at the same time initiating them gradually into those formulations of faith (prayers, hymns, creeds) that will permit them to participate in parish liturgy. Parents should be sensitive to the fundamental human and Christian equality of children as persons and honor this by genuine attention to their faith and insights and by occasionally giving them leadership roles.

Moments of passage (for example, the changing periods of ordinary adult development, new moments in the lives of the children such as graduation from school, points of dramatic transition such as change of job) are specially appropriate for family liturgies which, as far as possible, should be a natural part of the family's celebration of such occasions. These liturgies should serve also to insert these passages into the lifelong process of the person's initiation into the mystery of Christ's death and resurrection.

Significant success or failure by one or other family member can also be an occasion that calls for family prayer or even a more structured home liturgy that expresses gratitude or seeks guidance and hope.

Family worship, especially more detailed home liturgies, should lead to fuller sharing in parish liturgy by acquainting members of the family with the basic elements of Christian liturgy: hearing and responding to the scriptural word, awareness of the presence of Christ in a gathered community, expressing individual and group needs for divine help. It should also accustom them to active involvement in the liturgical action. Conversely, parish liturgy should help initiate people into those patterns of relating to God in Christ, which can then find more informal and diversified expression in family worship.

As an essential element of Christian catechesis, family liturgies should clarify the nature of discipleship in the concrete context of the practical responsibilities and ministerial possibilities of family members. They should also provide the occasion for persons to commit themselves to specific courses of Christian service.

A process of education and training of clergy and laity is needed to achieve these goals. There must be a greater appreciation of the need for and the role of home liturgies in developing the faith of individual members and of the family as a group. This will demand some understanding of the special character and flexible pluralism of family worship, worship that will often take forms that authentically ritualize the family's life but bear little resemblance to official liturgical activity.

There must also be increased acceptance, even encouragement, of the participation of Christian families *as families* in Christian ministry and in parish liturgy. Without such shared experience it is unrealistic to expect people to understand how their daily family life relates to the wider life of the Christian community.

Family liturgies should be the primary agent for integrating the individuals' life stories and the life story of the family (its own accumulating memories as well as its inherited family traditions) into the Christ-story that is being lived out in the Church.

LITURGY FOR CELEBRATING CHRISTIAN MARRIAGE

Kathleen Fischer and Thomas Hart

The wedding liturgy that follows is designed as a sacramental ritual in its own right rather than as a series of parts incorporated into a Eucharistic celebration. Depending upon such variables as the wishes of the couple or their families, the extent to which those in attendance will grasp the symbolic link of marriage and the Eucharist, or the custom in a given parish, the marriage liturgy can be followed by the Eucharist, which begins with the presentation of the gifts. However, the wedding liturgy is constructed to stand on its own as a sacramental celebration of Christ's abiding and transforming presence.

The liturgy is divided structurally into four elements: an introductory rite and three rites of passage. The introductory rite serves to welcome those in attendance and to recollect Christ's risen presence. Each of the rites of passage is meant to take account of the insights into the nature and needs of a new marriage given to us by the social and behavioral sciences, but to do so in the deeper context of Christian faith. Specifically, each rite situates the human realities of marriage within the central Christian mystery of Jesus' death and resurrection.

One of the primary functions of this liturgy is to teach the Christian understanding of marriage, but care must be taken not to overwhelm people with words or with theological sophistication. Effective symbolic actions have equal or greater impact. Commentary and prayers are best kept brief and to the point.

A fundamental principle governing this liturgical celebration is that the suggested ritual form here provided can and should be adapted to the particular situation. For example, the commentaries on each Scripture passage replace the homily, but a homily can be inserted after the Scripture reading in the Third Rite of Passage if circumstances warrant.

No specific suggestions are made for music, but there are several points in the liturgy when song would be an appropriate way for the assembly to participate: for example, at the beginning, during the exchange of peace, as the bridge and groom light their candles from the paschal candle, during the blessing of the couple, and in response to the Gospel.

Rite of Christian Marriage

ENVIRONMENT

If possible, the ceremony is held in a fairly large open space, where participants can sit in a semi-circle around the central action. It need not take place in a church building, especially if the space available in the church would impede the sense of *people* being gathered together to celebrate.

Prominent symbolic objects include the book for Scripture readings, candles, flowers, and a banner or two announcing the themes of Christian marriage. The paschal candle stands unlit before the assembly, flanked by stands for the candles that bride and groom will place there. Candles for the bride and groom and the assembly are readily available.

To avoid lengthy commentaries during the celebration, a simple printed program is provided to explain the basic structure of the liturgy and to provide whatever information, directions, and music people will need.

Introductory Rites

ENTRANCE

The bride and groom may enter in procession joined by parents and attendants.

GREETING

The bride and groom greet the assembly. Their greeting may include a brief word of welcome and the introduction of significant participants such as parents, witnesses, including the witnessing priest, and musicians.

The bride and groom stand to one side of the paschal candle, facing the people. The priest-witness comes forward to address the assembly.

Priest: We gather today in the presence of the risen Christ.
His passage from the darkness of death
to the glory of the resurrection
burns here in our midst as a beacon of hope:
the pledge that his love abides with us;
the promise that his light goes before us;
the sign that his power redeems us.

A family member or friend lights the candle.

Priest: We who rekindle this Easter flame
and gather around its light
stand as a sign of Christ's presence in the world.
We are his body,
entrusted with his promise:
where two or three pray in his name
Christ himself is present.

We gather to bless God
for the gift of N. and N. in our midst.
In their entry into the new life of marriage
they reveal anew
the mystery of Christ's death and resurrection in us,
that through our sharing in his death we come to life.
By the power of their love for one another,
they reveal the mystery of Christ present in his body,
made of many members,
bearing different gifts,
joined as one in love.

As we are a sign of Christ's presence with us,
so we are a sign of Christ's presence to them
as they begin this journey of new life together.

Let us ask God, source of life and love, to bless them:

All: God, our loving creator,
your care has led N. and N. on their journey
of deeper love and care for one another.
Strengthen them today
as they celebrate and pledge their commitment
to one another and to you.
Bless them as they continue to journey together.
Through them bless your people.

First Rite of Passage:
Leave-taking and New Bonding of Family and Friends

Bride and groom go to sit with their respective families or, in the absence of family, with close friends.

PROCLAMATION OF THE WORD

Before the Scripture reading, a parent or friend comments on:
—the place of leave-taking from family and friends in the marriage commitment;
—the primacy of the marital relationship and its effect on all other relationships;
—the entry into marriage as dying and rising, related to the paschal mystery and the biblical journey of faith.

Suggested Scripture readings are:

Gen 1:26-28, 31a
Gen 2:18-24

> Ruth 1:16-17
> Cant 2:10-14, 16

ESTABLISHMENT OF NEW RELATIONSHIPS

At the conclusion of the reading, the bride and groom leave their families of origin and join one another in front of the assembly.

Each says to the other:

> *N.*
> I want to share my family and friends with you.
> I want you to come to know and love them as I do,
> and to receive life from them as I have.

Bride and groom then invite families and friends to greet one another in peace and friendship.

Second Rite of Passage: Establishment of the New Marriage

PROCLAMATION OF THE WORD

Witnesses come forward and join bride and groom in front of the assembly. One of the witnesses comments on:
—the value of love in Christian life;
—the sacramental nature of married love;
—marriage as an image of the relationship of Christ to the Church.

Suggested Scripture readings are:

> Eph 3:14-21
> Col 3:12-17
> 1 John 4:7-12
> Matt 5:13-16
> Matt 22:35-40
> John 2:1-11
> John 10:11-15
> John 15:3-11
> John 15:12-17

PLEDGE OF COMMUNITY SUPPORT

The priest-witness addresses the people:

Priest: Will you support *N.* and *N.* in their new life together,
rejoicing in their happiness
and sustaining them in times of hardship?

All: R︎. We will.

Priest: Will you be patient and forgiving
when they make mistakes or cause pain? R⁄.

Will you pray for them
and ask God's blessing on their journey? R⁄.

EXCHANGE OF MARRIAGE VOWS

Bride and groom exchange vows.

Suggested forms are:

Option A: N.,
I choose you to be my husband (wife).
I promise to be faithful to you forever,
to love you in your joys and sorrows,
to comfort and challenge you
during all our days together.
In taking you as my husband (wife),
I accept one of God's greatest gifts to me.

Option B: N.,
I take you for my husband (wife).
I promise to love you faithfully
all the days of my life.
I want my love to mirror Christ's love for you,
true, patient, kind, self-sacrificing,
in good times and in bad,
a creative and renewing force in your life.
Together with you,
I want to grow in the life we share
as followers of Jesus Christ.

BLESSING AND EXCHANGE OF RINGS

If the baptismal font is nearby, water is taken from it to bless the
rings, signifying that marriage is a living out of baptism.

Priest:

Option A: Lord, bless these rings,
symbols of the enduring love which N. and N. offer
one another.

Option B: May the Lord bless these rings.
May they remind you of the permanence of the love
you promise today.
May you live it out in the daily paschal mystery of
dying and rising with steadfastness and joy.

Bride and groom exchange rings, saying:

> *N.*, accept this ring as a sign of our marriage.
> May it always remind you of my love for you.

Bride and groom are given unlit candles, which they light together in the flame of the paschal candle and then place in the holders on either side of the paschal candle stand.

Bride and groom kiss. The priest-witness pronounces them married. The assembly applauds.

Blessing of the Couple by the People

Bride and groom kneel. The priest-witness invites the people, or representatives if the assembly is large, to come forward and lay hands on the couple in silent blessing as an expression of their support and prayer.

After laying on hands, the people or their representatives form a circle around the couple. A representative of the group says the prayer of nuptial blessing:

Option A: May God bless you, *N.* and *N.*,
and give you long years of joy in one another.
May your union of love be life-giving
and enable you to offer help and comfort to all who come to you.

Option B: God, you created humankind in your image as woman and man.
Bless this union of *N.* and *N.* as husband and wife.
Give them your grace
that they may live in faithful friendship with one another forever.
Open their hearts to all in need,
and let others find in their love for one another
a sign of your love for all people.

Third Rite of Passage: Sacrament to the World

Proclamation of the Word

The priest-witness comments on:
— the call of all Christians to holiness and to involvement in the labor of Christ in the world;
— the corresponding call of *N.* and *N.* to serve and to live the paschal mystery and the values of the Gospel.

Suggested Scripture readings are:

Matt 5:1-10
Matt 5:13-16
Matt 25:31-46
Luke 10:25-37
John 15:12-17

Ordinarily, the commentaries before the readings replace a homily, but if desired, a homily following the readings relates the various parts of the liturgy to the basic meaning of Christian marriage.

After the reading, bride and groom take up their candles.

RESPONSE TO THE GOSPEL CHALLENGE

Couple: We publicly acknowledge our responsibility as
            Christians,
                and we freely choose to live the values of the Gospel
                in our home, our relationships to people, and our
                service to those in need.
            We see our particular gifts to be . . . . (Here they
                mention two or three areas in which they can serve
                others, either as individuals or as a couple.)
            In our Christian lives, we especially wish to devote
                our energies and resources to . . . . (Here they
                identify one or two service activities in which they
                plan to engage.)
            And now, as we spread the light of Christ to all of you,
                we invite you in silent prayer to renew your own
                Christian commitment
            to serve your brothers and sisters.

Bride and groom begin to light the assembly's candles from their own. As the light spreads, all silently make their own response to the gospel challenge.

Concluding Rites

(If the liturgy of the Eucharist follows, the concluding rites are omitted.)

GENERAL INTERCESSIONS

A member of the assembly invited by the bride and groom leads the intercessions.

Leader: For *N.* and *N.,*

that they may come to know in their life together
the height and depth and breadth of Christ's love
and the fullness of his life,
let us pray to the Lord.

All: ℟. Favor them, O Lord, with happiness and peace.

Leader: For their families,
their sisters and brothers,
and especially for their parents,
in thanksgiving for the years of love and support
   evident this day,
let us pray to the Lord. ℟.

That divisions among nations, sexes, religions, races,
may be healed through the power of Christian love,
and that this marriage may ever be a sign to all of
   that power,
let us pray to the Lord. ℟.

SONG

Bride and groom invite the assembly to join them in a song of commitment and celebration. After the song, the couple asks everyone to extinguish their candles and take them home as a remembrance.

DISMISSAL

Bride and groom invite the people to continue the celebration at the reception and, where appropriate, lead the way to the reception.

Liturgy of the Eucharist

If the liturgy of the Eucharist follows the marriage liturgy, the *Third Rite of Passage* is followed by the preparation of the altar and gifts. This preparation is led by the bride and groom and those they have invited to participate. They may use some of their own belongings: candles, bread and wine, plate and goblets, table cloth, and any other appropriate symbols of their own lives. They and others they invite assist in the distribution of Communion.

The nuptial blessing has already taken place and therefore is not repeated in its traditional place after the Lord's Prayer. The special blessing of bride and groom is also omitted from the concluding rites and the usual blessing used instead. After the blessing the couple invites everyone to continue the celebration at the reception and leads the way out.

The Eucharistic liturgy focuses less on this particular couple than on the community at large and the all-embracing themes of love, marriage, covenant, and service. Texts are provided here for the prayer over the gifts, the preface, and the prayer after communion:

PRAYER OVER THE GIFTS

Option A: Lord, accept these gifts we offer you.
With them we offer ourselves.
May we daily be drawn into closer union with you and one another.
Grant this through Christ our Lord.

Option B: Lord, we bring our gifts
and with them we offer ourselves.
Help us live out what we symbolize here,
with trust in you and generous love for our brothers and sisters.
We ask this in the name of Jesus Christ our Lord.

PREFACE

Option A: We praise and thank you, O Lord,
for you are a God of covenant with your people.
Through your covenant with Israel
you revealed the meaning of love and fidelity
in the face of waywardness and infidelity.
Still more generous is your new and eternal covenant
in your Son Jesus Christ.
You ask husband and wife to love one another
as Christ loves the Church,
with a self-giving love
that is faithful to death.
We thank you for the gift of marriage,
the sign of your enduring love for your people
and the symbol of your everlasting presence in our midst.
We celebrate your covenant of love
as we sing:
Holy, holy, holy . . . .

Option B: Praise to you, O God,
for creating man and woman in your image
and rejoicing in the beauty and goodness of your creation.

We praise you, O God,
for calling woman and man to care for all creation
and for entrusting them to one another
as companions in this task.
We praise you, O God,
for giving us the gift of human love,
through which your graciousness touches our lives
as comfort and as challenge.
We praise you for all your gifts
as we sing:
Holy, holy, holy . . . .

PRAYER AFTER COMMUNION

Option A: Lord, we have broken the bread of life
and shared this meal in memory of Jesus the Christ.
As the grains of wheat and the grapes are many,
yet one in this bread and wine,
make us all one through our love for each other.
Grant this through Christ our Lord.

Option B: Lord, may our breaking of this bread
and drinking of this cup
strengthen our unity with one another
and make us faithful signs of your love.
We ask this in the name of Jesus Christ.

A SAMPLE FAMILY LITURGY:
CELEBRATION OF PRESENCE

William Roberts

Let us imagine a family with three children: six, eight, and ten
years old. The second child will make First Communion in two
weeks. The intent of the liturgy, then, is to make an explicit link
with the Sunday celebration of the Eucharist in the parish by evoking

an awareness of the family members' presence for one another and then relating this experience to Christ's presence in their midst at home and at the Eucharist.

Prior to the celebration, bread and wine (grape juice) are made ready in the kitchen. They will be used not to celebrate a pseudo-eucharist but to relate the sharing of bread and wine to the presence of Christ, thus helping the children to understand that the sharing of bread and wine at the Sunday Eucharist is a mystery of presence and not a matter of magical change.

A candle and matches are placed on the family table or on a small living room table around which the family will gather. If the baptismal candle of the child preparing for First Communion has been kept, this candle should be used. The family Bible and a glass for each family member are also placed on the table.

The mother and father are envisioned as co-presiders at this celebration. In a single-parent household, that parent assumes all of the roles assigned to either.

Opening

LIGHTING THE CANDLE

The child about to receive First Communion lights the candle.

One of the parents reminds the children that the Easter candle is used in the parish church as a symbol of the presence of the risen Christ in our midst; similarly, the family candle reminds us of Christ's presence in the home.

PRAYER

Mother: Let us pray:

Lord, on the night before you died,
you gave your friends bread and wine
as a sign that you wanted to be with us always
and to give yourself to us in love
so that we could have new life.

We pray today
that as we share together this food and drink
we may be aware that you are here with us;
that we may care for one another in love;
and that we may bring new life to one another
by sharing your life.
We ask this in your name, Lord Jesus Christ.

All: Amen.

SONG

A song expressing Christ's love for us is sung.

Word Sharing

READING: 1 Cor 11:23-25

The oldest child introduces the reading in these or similar words:

> In the first reading, St. Paul tells us how at the Last Supper Jesus gave bread and wine to his disciples as a sign that he was giving himself as a friend to them and to us.

The oldest child then reads the passage.

COMMENT

The mother comments in these or similar words:

> Let us remember that the risen Jesus is present here with us, even though we cannot see him. He still gives himself to us as our friend, just as he did to his disciples at the Last Supper.

RESPONSE: John 14:1, 18; 15:7, 9, 11-12

The mother reads the verses of the response.

All: R℣. I will not leave you orphans;
              I will come back to you.

READING: 1 Cor 13:4-8

The father introduces the reading in these or similar words:

> In the next reading, St. Paul describes some of the important characteristics of love.

The father then reads the passage.

REFLECTION

The father introduces a period of silent reflection in these or similar words:

> Let us think for a moment how we can grow in one of the ways mentioned in this reading.

Table Sharing

Preparation

The youngest child goes to the kitchen, brings back the bread and wine (grape juice), and puts them on the table.

Blessing

Father: Bless us, Lord,
as we now share this food and drink
so that we may be a blessing for one another.
We ask this in your name.

All: Amen.

Meal Sharing

A small helping of wine or grape juice is poured for each family member, but no one drinks yet.

The loaf of bread is passed around the table. Each member of the family in turn takes the bread and says a spontaneous prayer which may express thanksgiving, petition, and/or the promise of love for other members of the family. After the prayer, the person breaks off a piece of bread and passes the loaf to the next person.

When the last person has taken the bread and said a prayer, everyone eats and drinks.

Silent Reflection

One of the parents reminds the children of Christ's presence with them and invites everyone to join in silent reflection.

Prayer

All join in saying together a prayer such as the Prayer of St. Francis, the Lord's Prayer, or the doxology.

Sign of Peace

All exchange some sign of peace and affection.

Closing

Song

A closing song celebrating God's presence is sung.

Index

Adam and Eve, 43, 44
Adult development, 17
Augustine, St., 38, 39, 43–44

Baptism, 51, 63
Barbach, Lonnie, 28
Bernard, Jesse, 23–24
Bible, sexism and equality in, 23, 25, 55–57
Birth control, 39
bonum prolis, 38, 42

Canticle of Canticles, 35
Celibacy, 27, 37, 48
Change, effect on marriage commitment, 18–19
Christian marriage. See Marriage, Christian
Church
    eschatological significance of, 49
    as sacrament of Christ, 61
    sexism in, 54
Co-habitation, 29–30
Commitment, marriage, 18–19
Common law marriages, 38–39
Consummation, 37, 39, 41–42
Cosmic evolution and theology, 16
Council of Trent, 38, 41
Covenant, 35, 54
Culture and technology, 17–18

Divorce, 18, 26

Equality
    biblical basis for, 25, 55–57
    in family liturgies, 72
    in marriage, 23–25, 53–54
    in New Testament times, 56–57

in Old Testament times, 54–55
in wedding liturgies, 71
Erikson, Erik, 17
Eschatology of marriage, 47–49, 63
Eucharist and wedding liturgies, 41, 69, 70–71, 73–74, 81–83

Faith
    a context for marriage, 30–31
    development in family liturgies, 73
    in family life, 50
Family (see also Family, Christian)
    arrangements of marriage, 35, 36
    influence of members in, 20–21
    liturgies, 72–73, 83–86
    members as instruments of God, 21
    of origin, 21–22
    relationships, 19
    sexism in, 23
    therapy, 19–20
Family, Christian
    as a community of faith, 50
    described as a domestic Church, 49–50
    eschatological significance of, 49
    responsibility toward society of, 52–53
    Second Vatican Council on, 49
    sharing in Christ's mission, 51
    and worship, 50–51
Fidelity, 35, 36, 44, 48
Fiorenza, Elisabeth Schüssler, 56
First Vatican Council, 49

Gaudium et spes, 57
Generativity, a modern view of, 27

Hugh of St. Victor, 44
Human person, change and relation
    in, 15–16
Human sciences
    input in theology, 47
    insights on sexuality, 57
    research on marriage, 59–60
    in sacramental rituals, 9–10
    and wedding rituals, 74
Human sexuality
    an accepted subject, 28
    in Christian marriage today, 59
    in early Christian thinking, 35,
        36–37, 43, 44
    equality in, 29
    human sciences on, 57
    Second Vatican Council and,
        28–29
    sexual communication, focus on,
        28
    sexual dissatisfaction, seeking help
        for, 29
Hunger, family responsibility for, 29

Indissolubility of marriage, 41–42, 44

John Paul II, Pope, 52
Judaism, influence on Christian
    marriage, 35
Juridical view of Christian marriage,
    58

Krantzler, Mel, 17

Levinson, Daniel, 17
Life-styles and marriage, 29–30
Love and marriage, 48, 49, 58, 61,
    71

Mackin, Theodore, 59
Marriage (see also Marriage,
    Christian)
    common law, 38–39
    concerns surrounding, 12
    death and resurrection in, 19
    definitions of, 33–34
    distinguished by legal
        arrangements, 39

family of origin and, 21–22
and human sciences, 59–60
interdependence in, 19
and personal fulfillment, 25–26
roles and responsibilities in, 24–25
and selflessness, 26–27
sexism in, 54
stages of growth in, 17
and women's movement, 23–24
Marriage, Christian (see also
    Marriage, Christian, Catholic
    development of)
    benefits of historical reflection, 33
    equality in, 53–54
    eschatological nature of, 47–49, 63
    and fidelity, 48
    as an intimate partnership, 57–59
    juridical view of, 58
    love in, 48–49, 58, 61
    personal development in, 58
    preparation for, 30
    as a process, 49
    sacramentality of, 19, 60–63
    self-giving in, 63
    and sexuality, 59
    a shared experience, 59
    support, need for, 30–31
Marriage, Christian, Catholic
    developments of,
    blessings, 40
    Church and state involvement, 36,
        38–39, 40, 41–42
    common law marriages, 38–39
    consummation, 37, 39, 41–42
    contractual view, 37–38, 39, 41
    differences between the classes,
        35–36, 37–38
    distinguishing factors, 42
    economic arrangements, 37
    emergence of monasticism, 36–37
    Eucharistic celebrations, 41
    family arrangements, 35–36
    fidelity, 35, 36, 44
    indissolubility, 41–42, 44
    individuals as the effective agents,
        41
    influences of Judaism, 35
    influences of the Middle Ages,
        37–38, 41

influences of the Patristic period, 36–37, 43
influences of Roman law and custom, 35–36
influences of Teutonic peoples, 37
involvement of society, 37
official Church witness, 38–39
ordained minister, role of, 41
original sin, 43, 44
personalistic view, 40, 45
procreation, 35, 36, 38, 39, 40, 42, 44, 45
public marriage ceremony, 39
related to the love of Christ for his Church, 35, 36, 40–41, 42–43, 44–45
romantic love, 39
sacramentality of marriage, 38, 39, 41, 42–45
Second Vatican Council, 40, 45
sexism, 35
sexuality, 35, 36, 37, 38, 43, 44
decree *Tametsi* of the Council of Trent, 41
Marriage rituals, sexism in, 23
Medical science and reproduction, 27
Men, roles of, 24
Mental illness and family therapy, 19
Middle Ages, influence on marriage, 37–38, 41
Ministry of healing, family responsibility in, 52–53
Mission
of the Church, 61
of the family, 51–53, 73
individual, 71
Monasticism, 36–37
Music in wedding liturgies, 74
mysterion, 42, 43

Oppression, human, family responsibility toward, 53
Original sin, 43, 44

Parents, spiritual responsibility of, 49
Parish liturgy and the family, 51, 72-73
Patristic judgments, 36, 38

Patristic period, influences in marriage, 36–37, 43
Prayer, 12, 51, 72
Process thought, themes of, 15–16
Procreation, 27, 35, 36, 38, 39, 40, 42, 44, 45, 71
Psychoanalysis, 19–20
ratum, 41
Rite of passage, marriage and family and, 71, 72
Ritual, 10
Ritual, wedding. *See* Wedding rituals, suggestions for
Roman Catholic Church, 18, 28–29
Roman law, influence on marriage, 35–36

Sacraments, 9–10, 60–61
sacramentum, 42, 44
Salvation, 62
Second Vatican Council, 28–29, 40, 45, 49, 52, 57–58
Sexism
in the Church, 54
in the Bible, 23, 55
in marriage, 35, 54
in wedding rituals, 23
Sexuality, human. *See* Human sexuality
Sheehy, Gail, 17
Sin, 62, 63
Single life-style, 29
Social needs and family responsibility, 52–53
Systems model of marriage and family, 19

Tametsi, decree, 41
Technology and culture, 17–18
Teilhard, Pierre, de Chardin, 15–16
Teutonic peoples, influence on marriage, 37
Theology and cosmic evolution, 16

Vatican Council, First. *See* First Vatican Council
Vatican Council, Second. *See* Second Vatican Council
Vocation, Christian, 52

Wedding rituals, suggestions for,
  community support, 70, 71–72
  concluding rites, 80–81
  the couple in the key role, 69
  environment, 74
  Eucharistic celebrations, 69, 70–71,
    73–74, 81–83
  family involvement, 70
  First Rite of Passage, 76–77
  homily, 69–70, 71, 74, 80
  human sciences and, 74
  idea of mission, 71
  incorporating death/new life
    mystery, 71
  intimate friends, involvement of,
    70
  introductory rite, 74, 75–76
  Kingdom of God, theme of, 71
  love and intimacy, 71
  metaphors, use of, 72
  music, 74
  non-sexist language, use of, 71
  ordained minister, role of, 69–70
  printed program, 75
  a rite of passage, 71
  Second Rite of Passage, 77–79
  self-giving as central theme, 70
  symbolism, use of, 74–75, 81
  Third Rite of Passage, 79–80
Whitehead, Alfred North, 15–16, 19
Women
  treatment of, 54–57
  roles of, 24
Women's movement, 23–24
World peace, family responsibility
  in, 53
Worship, 50–51, 53 (see also Family
  liturgies)

Zilbergeld, Bernie, 28